With
gra Sur

The Power of
Owning Your Career
*Winning Strategies, Tools
and Tips for Creating Your
Desired Career!*

SIMONE E. MORRIS

Simone Morris
ENTERPRISES LLC
———• ESTABLISHED 2015 •———

www.simonemorris.com
smorris@simonemorris.com

DEDICATION

For my daughter, Mildred. You are the sunshine in my days. I strive to create a path that you can follow to be successful in all you endeavor to do.

CONTENTS

FOREWORD

I met Simone at a Greater Stamford Toastmasters meeting many years ago. We effortlessly became co-mentors – providing feedback and holding each other accountable on our parallel speaking and leadership journeys. I was privileged to watch Simone grow from a solid amateur to a seasoned professional speaker who commands the room not only with expertise but also with deep empathy.

In addition, Simone and I struck up a friendship while we joined forces in planning two TEDxMillRiver events. I was honored when Simone sought my guidance on how to write and publish her first book. Moreover, I was thrilled that Simone reached out to me years later to tell me that she'd written and published *Achievement Unlocked: Strategies to Set Goals and Manifest Them.*

Now, here we are as she gets ready to publish her second book. Here's what I know about Simone. She has been very hands-on in her journey. She does not just let life happen; she took command of her career in a way few of us are brave enough to do. After an amazing run as an information technology professional, she followed her passion by switching careers into diversity and inclusion. She's made a name for herself as a thought leader. She's authentic to the core, openly sharing her ups and downs with those of us following her on LinkedIn.

In *The Power of Owning Your Career*, Simone reveals her formula for assuming the driver's seat on your professional path. She delves into ensuring clarity on your career goals by working through a solid plan, putting strategic partnerships in place, and highlighting the importance of creating a personal brand. She showcases inspiring stories and relevant advice from leaders she interviewed for the book. I know you are in for a treat and will be able to start owning your own career with the immediately actionable advice Simone provides.

Jeremey Donovan
Author of "How to Deliver a TED Talk"

ACKNOWLEDGMENTS

I would like to acknowledge my honey, Stephen, for his continued support of all my goals and for all the love he gives to our family. Babe, thank you for believing in me.

I would like to acknowledge my family and friends for their continued support in all my career pursuits. You consistently stand and clap for me and I'm so grateful for your encouragement and belief in me. I appreciate you all. I would like to give a special shout out to my sister Michelle and my niece Ayanna for always going above and beyond to support my goals. I like to think of you two as the head of my family Public Relations firm. I love that we are able to come together and always support one another. Thank you both for already helping me to plan the book launch celebration party. I know it will be beyond amazing and truly memorable.

I would like to acknowledge all the wonderful people who allowed me to interview them and glean their wonderful career advice. The interviewees include David Kim, Mohammed Murad, Joseph Santana, Nancy Di Dia, Harry Rilling, John Lahey, Malaika Myers, Havilah Malone, Laura Skander-Trombley, Deb Dagit, Eric Pliner, Marc Stephenson Strachan, Tomiko Fraser-Hines and Clyde Tinnen. Thank you for authentically sharing your stories and wisdom with me. Thank you for your patience in the process. It was truly my pleasure to work with all of you.

I would like to thank Jeremey Donovan for the wonderful foreword. He has always been very supportive and I'm grateful to consider him a friend.

A big thank you to those who took the time out to endorse the book. That includes Bridgett McGowen-Hawkins, Heneka Watkis-Porter, Lucy Sorrentini and Jeff Davis. Thank you for endorsing my work. I'm so grateful.

I would like to thank my assistant, Jen, for her support while I completed this book. She was instrumental in coordinating the interviews and follow-ups that I needed. Thank you, Jen. Your help was invaluable.

I would like to acknowledge my accountability partners for this book. They popped in and dropped a dose of empowerment, always encouraging me to keep going for the home stretch by fully owning my accountability. Thank you! You know who you are!

I would like to thank my Rockstar graphic designer, Kim, for all the great work she continues to do for me. You're a million miles away but you always deliver on the vision and so I remain a fan and am super grateful.

I would like to thank my editor, Catherine. Your input has been valuable and worthwhile to me as I launched my second book into the world.

I would also like to thank Danielle Robinson. Working for her was enlightening. One day, when we were having a career conversation, I must have been complaining or demonstrating lack of ownership because she proclaimed, "You are responsible for your career." That message stuck with me because it was delivered at the right time and it was the confirmation I needed to move forward with getting into the driver's seat instead of allowing others to create my path.

I'm proud that today, I'm very hands-on in the trajectory for my career.

Lastly, I would like to thank the Simone Morris Enterprise LLC Community. These are the people who engage with me through social media. Thank you for allowing me to share my true self and for always cheering me on. I appreciate you so much.

BOOK PRAISE

Revealing, poignant, honest, and eye-opening. Simone takes hugely brave steps with sharing her personal career trajectory, detailing a balance of risks, failures, and triumphs in her life before college and beyond. As such, novice and seasoned professionals alike are sure to experience multiple ah-ha moments. You will reminisce, you will smile, and you will clearly see not just what it means to take control of your career but, most importantly, WHY you must do so!

Bridgett McGowen
Award-Winning International Professional Speaker
www.bridgettmcgowen.com

***

No matter where you are in your own career trajectory *The Power of Owning Your Career* is a must-read for professionals who are interested in creating an authentic and passionate career trajectory. The stories Simone shares both inspire and empower the reader to take ownership and action to create a career they are both passionate about and responsible for. Kudos to you, Simone, for challenging us to craft our own narrative and create the career of our dreams.

Lucy Sorrentini
Founder and CEO, Impact Consulting, LLC Diversity & Inclusion Strategist, Executive Coach
http://www.impactconsultingus.com

The Power of Owning Your Career is a must read if you've ever felt powerless about the direction in which your career is going. If you already 'have it together', read it to keep inspired on your journey. It's not just another motivational book; Simone shares practical tips that you can implement immediately to propel you in the direction of your win.

Heneka Watkis-Porter
Entrepreneur, Author, Podcaster & Speaker
henekawatkisporter.com

***

In *The Power of Owning Your Career*, you'll find a practical guide to steering your life in the direction you truly desire and reaching your version of success. Simone authentically shares her own story while mixing in powerful case studies and relevant examples. If you're looking to take your career to the next level, read this book.

Jeff Davis, CEO, Jeff Davis International
Author, *The Power of Authentic Leadership*
jeffdspeaks.com

.

INTRODUCTION

The power of owning your career is a concept that really resonated with me in my last year as an employee in Corporate America. I had worked at a company for a few years shy of two decades. It was a pretty good run. I had great pay and benefits, and great people to work with, but something was missing. This job allowed me opportunities to travel the world with and without the company. It allowed me friendships that felt more like being part of a family. In essence, I was comfortable and complacent.

Truth be told, I knew that it was time to leave but I was scared to leave "home," so to speak. It was like that feeling you get when you are going off to college and you are scared to leave the comforts you're accustomed to. I wondered what had happened to that brave girl who used to job hop in her younger years to find the best opportunity. Somehow I had lost her along the way. I had grown up and I was remembering and living lessons my mother instilled in me about being responsible. I was being a responsible adult and therefore, I had achieved the proverbial stability with a good job. And that's where the story should end, right? At least, that's the story I sold to myself. I sought stability to ensure I had the lifestyle I desired. And I had a pretty good one that I didn't want to jeopardize.

God surely knew that I wasn't following his plan and so he put some pretty big signs in my way. To stop the clock and allow myself the time to think about what's next, I took an unpaid sabbatical from work. I should mention that it came about because I was on the verge of quitting. I needed a shakeup and I had a sit down with a human resource business partner. She wanted to know what was going on with me. Internally, I screamed, "I'm going no place in this company. I'm unhappy but I have a good job. I have to stay. Where am I going to find another good job like this one? Arrrrrgggghhhhhh!" But of course, I did not say that. I instead asked for a time-out and by God, I was granted it.

A sabbatical is a period of time when an employee takes a leave of absence from their job. In some instances, these are paid leaves, but in this instance it was an unpaid leave. This can be a scary thing to do but at the time, I was single, and so I had a bit more flexibility in making the decision. In my opinion, sabbaticals breathe life into the weary. It gives you the time to say, "What the heck am I doing here?" It allows you time to slow down and smell the roses again. It was something I desperately needed to do. Some folks thought I was on extended vacation, while others thought, *That chick is crazy!* But you know what, I continued. I had to begin the process of filling my tank back up. Somehow the fuel gauge was sticking on an extended empty and hadn't been repaired in quite some time.

My three-month sabbatical allowed me time to re-evaluate whether I could continue on this path. The time off was refreshing, renewing, and rejuvenating. My eyes were opened to the fact that I must have been put on the earth for a divine purpose, and try as I might to shrink back from the responsibility, I would never be at ease until I stepped into my greatness.

Here are some telling signs that you need to re-evaluate your career:

- When you dread getting up in the morning for work and you live for Fridays and holidays just to have a reprieve.
- When you know you're not valued or seen as a high-potential employee, yet you stay around hoping to enlighten others.
- You are uneasy but not willing to rock the boat.
- You accept zero to minimal responsibility for your career challenges.

It was while I was on sabbatical that I decided to invest in a coach to help me sort out the madness. I had to get clear on what was right for Simone. Frankly, I wasn't sure the technical world was my be-all-and-end-all. I had invested many years on that journey and I was at a turning point. I felt strongly that I was called to do more, so I decided to be a life coach. I had been giving people sage advice for many years without the formal training. Anyone undertaking the intensive training required to be a coach knows you get a magnifying glass out and you start looking at your life close up, so you can better understand yourself and really be impactful in coaching others. It was a life-changing, freeing experience. Before long, my sabbatical was ending and I was asked to return to work earlier than planned.

Things were moving along nicely, however, it wasn't long before I found myself yearning for more again. The message to me was simple. God doesn't let up until you listen.

Along the journey of discovering my next chapter, I was granted an opportunity to pour my creative talents into leading an internal employee resource group. I was still not fully owning my career because I had a passion for empowering women. I was advised that I would be of better service leading the minority group. Let me say here that this was one of my passenger moments and so I accepted the extracurricular role with gusto. And guess what happened? It breathed new life and passion into me. It was then that my intrapreneurial abilities started to surface. My leadership skills took the forefront. I was able to create a way out of no way. I was creating a brand that had a voice that was listened to. I was sitting down with senior leaders and voicing my opinion. I was speaking to 100 employees. Where did this person come from? It was a refreshing taste of the future. I wanted more of it. So, I became a driver. A real driver of change. And I was accelerating the pedal hard for success.

I was surprised by how much I enjoyed the work, even though I wasn't paid for it. When I dug deep, I determined that it was because I was able to create an impact. I was able to change culture and change lives. I was able to be seen and heard. It gave me a fire and passion. I could no longer sit idly as my career passed me by. I had choices and I had to use my voice to make them come to life.

The new Simone was more confident, took more risks, and let her voice be heard. She wasn't afraid to challenge the status quo. Unfortunately, that also meant challenging leaders. I did not have an appetite for bullshit. And this new Simone didn't have a problem asking the tough questions. It didn't win me any friends. I think I had resolved myself to the fact that I was not moving anywhere upwards in my day job. The silent message had been loud and clear and the difference was, the old Simone wasn't listening—the *new* Simone was listening. She decided that once she knew where she stood, she had to decide about what to do. She knew the time had come to leave her comfortable place and that is exactly what she did. On July 31, 2013, she officially closed her chapter as an employee in the corporate arena and begun a new, undefined chapter in life.

The slate was cleared. The opportunity was there for the taking. It was a chance to figure out who this new Simone was and who she wanted to be in life. For years, she had hidden behind a powerful brand and it was time for her to stand in the light of her very own brand. The only thing was, she didn't know what that brand was so she had to discover it. She became the true leader she was meant to be, understanding that she didn't know it all but that she was being guided to create an empowerment movement for women.

When I crafted the *Power of Owning Your Career* keynote, I shared my message with networking groups, community groups, and conferences around the country. Each time I delivered the keynote, it generated a lot of energy and the audience's feedback proved that there was an appetite for learning more. One example of this was delayed feedback I received from a conference attendee whom I met for the second time in another city at another conference.

As I got on the shuttle bus to transfer over to the New Orleans Convention Center, I noticed a woman who looked familiar to me. She must have felt the same way because she struck up a conversation, sharing how much she enjoyed my *Power of Owning Your Career* talk in Las Vegas. I was so mesmerized and inspired by her words that I asked her to take a minute to jot down her words as a testimonial for me. Here are her words:

> *Just want to say thank you! If it wasn't for your session, I wouldn't have had the confidence to ask for what I want in my contract with a client. The tips you gave were priceless and very helpful. I can't thank you enough.*
>
> *Angela Caraway, Owner, The Caraway Management Group*

It was clear that I had a worthwhile message deserving of expansion to provide deeper learning insights for a larger audience. It would, in fact, be this book that I had to share with the world.

In *The Power of Owning Your Career*, I will share my formula for successfully owning your career. I will also provide profiles from leaders at the top of their game who generously agreed to allow me to interview them to share their personal career stories and insights. I hope that this book will help you to step up from the passenger seat and provide you with the opportunity to recognize that you are indeed in full control of your career and you can in fact craft your own roadmap for success.

To sum it all up, this is a career management guidebook that outlines the importance of taking ownership of your career, gives you a formula for doing so, takes a deep dive into the behaviors you must assume to implement it, and profiles leaders from diverse industries who want to share their stories, advice, and mentorship with you.

1 THE NECESSITY OF CAREER OWNERSHIP

"Control your own destiny or someone else will."
- Jack Welch

When you start talking careers and ownership, ears perk up. Everyone is curious about learning something new that may give them a boost in the area of career management. We all know the answers, but somehow, we've been brainwashed into thinking someone else holds the keys. We think we are mere passive passengers waiting for our big break. I'm here to tell you that to have that powerful career, you need to step up and make it happen. I'm happy to take the journey with you because it's one I had to take myself. In essence, I had to experience the journey in order to walk the talk.

The ability to own your career shows up earlier than you might think. Perhaps you are unaware of the constant signs you ignore, as was the case for me. I continued ignoring signs that showed up after graduation from college. Disillusioned by the inability to pursue the path I thought I was passionate about, I acquiesced and got a job as a temporary clerical worker. It was a good job, albeit temporary, and I held it for more than a year. It was my first taste of a lucrative salary with as many perks as you could get from temporary work. I even accumulated enough credits to get a week's paid vacation. Back then, it was pretty exciting, even though I knew that this wasn't my end game. I expected more of myself as a college graduate.

My luck began to change when I got a job as a customer service representative (CSR) at a financial services firm. It was a full-time, permanent opportunity with nice benefits. I remember one of the key performance benefits was an option of either a bonus or a paid company vacation. I was giddy to take my first Carnival cruise as a perk from my job. I didn't last long as a CSR; I got a promotion as a coordinator in the internal training department.

It was during that time that I dipped my toe in the entrepreneurial waters by launching my first part-time business, *Creative Ventures*. The business was a mix of my creative talents plus my information technology training skills. Although I had a few clients, I did not gain enough momentum to transition this into a full-time business. Hence, I closed the business and continued moving forward with my work in the training profession. I was offered a role teaching adults computer software packages 16 times a month, and I jumped at the opportunity. It turned out to be a great learning experience. We shall call that Job Hop One.

From there, I landed another role as a database specialist at a paper company (Job Hop Two). This provided me the opportunity to get very technical. I undertook some on-the-job training and became certified in Lotus Notes. Back then, I was toying with the idea of continuing my higher education. I was lucky to receive encouragement from old professors and work colleagues to move forward with additional education. Hence, I enrolled for my MBA at the University of Connecticut with a concentration in Management of Technology.

Opportunities continued to avail themselves to me. I took an opportunity to continue growing in the technical space by accepting an application developer role at a technology company (Job Hop Three). I was whetting my appetite as a lifelong learner. I was beginning to garner evidence that my education was allowing me to jump forward in my career more than I did with on-the-job training. It became a passionate platform for me wherein I advocated the virtues of post-secondary education to move ahead in your career.

It worked because those moves allowed me to continue an upward migration from application developer, to senior application developer, to project manager, to technical project manager. After five years, I would move to my final corporate gig and end my job-hopping stint. I stayed with that company for more than 15 years (Job Hop Four).

After a while, one wants to settle down and get comfortable, so my job hopping became less attractive. I had no idea that so much time would pass. My longest tenure at a company was previously five years. In my mind, I thought I was doing pretty darn good! I had credibility, experience, and perks. But the time arrived when I wanted more. I just didn't know how to get it outside of the corporate environment; Perhaps I expected that I would get it within my current environment.

I was stumbling along, not accepting responsibility and wondering why the decision makers weren't recognizing my brilliance as I watched others move up the career ladder. I convinced myself that my situation wasn't too shabby. After all, I had a lot of flexibility with my tenure, a great salary and benefits, access to prestigious events, and products I enjoyed being a consumer for.

For me, it took many years and circumstances to highlight the clarity I desperately sought in my youth and to finally take ownership of my career. And even with that clarity, there were still learning moments when I challenged myself with my thinking.

I've had a wonderful career in Corporate America and now I am blessed to be continuing my career as an entrepreneur. Today, I'm the driver owning my career and my journey. However, the saboteurs—or gremlins if you will—challenge me at every turn. I highlight this because while you are going to learn lessons, tips, and tools to help you learn how to own your career, you will have to work constantly to retain ownership and to be the master of the mine field in your head. You will also have to fight potential naysayers who lack vision for your course. My advice to you is to stay positive, stay focused, stay in action, and stay in the moment.

I feel compelled to share my story to empower others by learning from those of us who are excelling in our careers. As such, I've provided an authentic look at diverse leaders and their respective journeys, knowing that their insights and wisdom will be helpful to those seeking guidance. There is a need to have a plan and to be proactive in seeking the education you do not know about. A fresh-eyed college student doesn't know what they need to know unless they have spent time understanding what they want and what they need before entering college. I was one of those students. I only knew that I wanted to be a buyer and that was it.

The same goes for Corporate America. With your upbringing, you are taught certain skills. So, there are indeed cultural differences. As a Black Jamaican woman, I was taught that it was important to have a roof over my head and a job to pay the bills, the importance of family, and to be careful in life (i.e. to be risk averse). Therefore, I found myself treading very carefully in my career. One example of this was saying no to career opportunities that called for relocation, especially if it wasn't in an area where I had close ties. I was also taught lessons about problem-solving and financial management. These lessons are so vital in owning your career. When you try to buck those lessons as you become enlightened and there is clarity in what you desire from life, you must be strong and you must be armed with a proactive plan to succeed. You must also have a winning team around you to ensure you have the right influences and accountability to succeed. There was much I needed to learn and I wish the learning curve could have been shorter. That my dear readers is what I want to help you with: a more direct path to career ownership.

Let's begin our journey to powerfully owning your career.

My definition of *career* is a body of work that spans a period of time that evokes passion and responsibility to succeed. Some mistake a job as a career. In some instances, I suppose it could be. Over the years, I have shifted from "just jobs" to a true career. I can see very clearly from the early days that I was not educated enough to claim and steer my own path. There are some defining moments that stand out for me.

1. Very early on, I had an inkling of becoming a teacher. When I shared it, my mom declared that there was no money in the profession. It occurs to me that I must have been convinced because I let that go by the wayside. It would take several years for me to realize that I was still being a teacher in the roles I played even if it wasn't the official title or as I originally imagined it to be.

2. My skinny frame always generated questions as to whether I might be a model or a basketball player. I had zero basketball skills and wanted to be a model. My mom said no, but this go around I said yes to that dream. Imagine, a young Simone racking up a sizeable credit card debt (while in college) to attend John Casablanca's Modeling School. I knew that I had it in me to be successful and that I'd prove my mom wrong. Needless to say, there was no return on that investment for this wannabe fashion model. #Next

3. I had no clue what I wanted to be when I grew up so I decided it would be a good idea to follow in the footsteps of my sisters and become a secretary. I was a bit concerned that it wouldn't come to fruition after getting a D in my typing class, however, I improved my typing skills and learned stenography. I was so good I received a scholarship award from Sacred Heart University. I was headed to secretarial school when my business teacher, Miss S., intervened,

causing my path to be forever shifted. She convinced me college was worth a try, so I applied to two schools and got into both. Imagine my surprise at this new possibility.

4. My major in college was Marketing with a concentration in Retail Management. I had aspirations of becoming a buyer. When I graduated from college and got rejected from the Macy's Leadership Development Program, I was devastated. That was my only plan of attack for success. I was so wounded it didn't occur to me to continue to try. It didn't even occur to me to ask for feedback on why I was rejected. After the disappointment wore off, I discovered that I had much more of an appetite for Computer Science and that career took off when I landed a position.

5. I recall doing well at a job when a boss approached me about taking a leadership role with two direct reports. I was flattered but I held back because a colleague had mentioned his interest to me in the role. I felt that I would be betraying him so I took a pass and he took the role.

6. I got comfortable in a job where I wasn't moving up the ladder but I was making good money and I enjoyed the benefits of the job. I stayed way too long. I knew that I had more to give, but I was afraid to step away from the safety net. Complacency is a beast that eats time.

The point I'm trying to make here is that I was a willing and able passenger for a very long time. I enjoyed it. I didn't have to challenge myself to make the tough decisions and I was ok with it. However, with time, I began to realize that something was missing and there was a path designed for me that I wasn't claiming. The feeling stayed with me until I embraced uncertainty and took a risk to reap greater rewards.

Perhaps there's an example from what I described above that you can relate to. I'm sure you must have your own examples that you can jot down as a point of reflection and reference.

When you take your hands off your career, others will put their hands on it and steer you in a direction that they perceive to be in your best interest. Until you can feel at your core that you are responsible for the direction and outcome of your career, you will remain under the control of someone else.

Take a look at LinkedIn and you'll see examples of those people driving their career in a direction that's favorable to them. You know the ones; you see them excelling in each career undertaking. They are in the news, they continue to move in an upward manner with increased responsibilities, they are running their own companies, etc. Brandwatch[1] cites a study that found 2/3 of millionaires use LinkedIn today. Now I will agree that some of it is perception. What I mean by perception is that there is a story that's being shared. Some call it branding. I learned long ago that perception is reality (even if it isn't). So, you have to do the due diligence to see whether there's truth and evidence to support the brand's claim. We can see examples of that now playing out in the media with folks who were undoubtedly

---

1 https://www.brandwatch.com/blog/linkedin-statistics/

at the top of their games but now they are spiraling downward for negative behaviors.

WHY IS IT IMPORTANT TO OWN YOUR CAREER?

It's important to take ownership of your career because there's a certain peace of mind that comes about as a result of knowing the vision you have for your career is unfolding in the manner you intended. When you don't participate in the movements of your career, you're basically saying, "It's not important to me." Someone else has made it a priority and they determine what your next steps are.

Consider the following scenario:

You are in a meeting with your boss for your annual performance review. The conversation begins with you presenting your wins to your boss and then your boss takes their turn sharing feedback from your customers. When your boss asks what future roles you're interested in, you don't have a good response. You're pretty exhausted from everything happening in your personal life and the fact that you stayed up way too late last night binge-watching the latest season of *This is Us*.

So, you say the first thing that comes to mind.

And that is . . . "I'm flexible."

What does that tell your boss?

It says, "We like her. She can fit where we need her." Just like that, you're off on a direction that's not necessarily where you want to go in your career.

Here's another scenario:

An entrepreneur (new in business) is finding that much happens through networking but is an introvert and would prefer buckling down with the nuts and bolts of their business. This entrepreneur believes that staying focused on the work will yield the profitable results they seek. The result is they're not making enough revenue to sustain their entrepreneurial pursuits.

What could the entrepreneur do differently to yield better revenue results?

In both scenarios, the individuals have an opportunity to adopt a more hands-on approach to undoubtedly yield better results with their influence and direction.

There are many ways in which success is tied to career ownership. Some examples of people who are doing it well include:
   1. Oprah Winfrey — Her success path consists of being a journalist to owning her own production studio to

literally owning her OWN network. I think we would all agree that from what we know about her and her trajectory, she is indeed a career maven who has successfully navigated and owned her career.

2. Magic Johnson — He went from basketball player to business mogul. Magic Johnson played for the Lakers, winning championships, and under the tutelage of his coach has gone on to be quite an impressive businessman on his way to billionairehood.

3. Beyoncé Knowles Carter — The fabulous and talented Beyoncé needs no last name even though we all know it. She has successfully parlayed herself from the group Destiny's Child to what is seemingly her birthright as a businesswoman. Whatever she touches turns to gold. Whether it's a clothing line, fragrance collection, acting in films, directing biopics, or releasing her Grammy-nominated albums without her record label all online, Beyoncé is another person who demonstrates that she can have the career she wants on her terms.

4. Elon Musk — Tesla, PayPal, and trips to space: This is what we think of when he hear "Elon Musk." He is one of those who has been admired for his continued successes. He's a mover and shaker and we eagerly watch for his next move.

5. Arianna Huffington — the founder and creator of the Huffington Post. One would think that the success that came from the Huffington Post was her be-all-and-end-all but Arianna shocked us all by moving on from her namesake company to create her next chapter with Thrive Global.

6. Steve Jobs — The late, great Steve Jobs was known for making Apple something more than a fruit and a device that most of us can't live without today. His

remarkable story of creating Apple Computers and being fired, reinventing himself and finding more successes and reclaiming ownership of his company makes him one of the greatest success stories of all time.

7. Marissa Mayer — At a young age, she created her own way from Google and moving on to head up Yahoo. Although there was much backlash from her stance on women having it all, she has still been ultra-successful on her own terms.

8. Corey Booker — From Mayor of New Jersey to Senator, Corey Booker has proven to be a likeable hero with an amazing following. Some say he's laying the groundwork to land in the White House.

9. Hilary Clinton — Hillary Clinton is masterful at navigating her career. And what a career she's had. From lawyer to First Lady of the White House to being Senator of New York and then on to becoming Secretary of State. Then she landed her highest position, being the Democratic Nominee for the United States presidency.

10. Sheryl Sandberg — She created a revolution, prompting women to lean in to their brilliance. As Chief Operating Officer of Facebook, author, and keynote speaker, she has taken the world by storm and created a global movement around empowering women.

11. Sir Richard Branson — As head of the Virgin conglomerate, Sir Richard is a billionaire who is willing to share his knowledge with the rest of us. From talking about his to-do lists and how they've come to pass, to vacationing with former President Obama, we know he's one cool dude.

12. Mark Cuban — Known for his winning personality as owner of the Dallas Mavericks, venture capitalist and star of ABC's *Shark Tank*, Mark Cuban demonstrates that he's authentically winning his career on his terms.
13. Jeff Bezos, CEO of Amazon — Everyone knows Amazon. It revolutionized the entire shopping process, allowing us to get much done from home. The brand that Jeff has created is amazing.
14. And more.

All these movers and shakers have some traits in common. They are all ambitious, driven, are able to get the job done, are risk takers, and so much more. We know they've all experienced challenges but they persevered and are at the top of their game.

In order to successfully manage our careers, keep the following in mind:

You can't play the game without keeping your eye on the score.
We must know where we stand in our careers at all times. This allows us to navigate the direction that we want to take for career success.

We must build and nurture the right relationships.
We must have the right relationships and partnerships in place. If we don't have them, we must seek them out and make them a reality.

We must be willing to seek out the opportunities that best meet our needs.
We must be diligent about seeking opportunities to stretch ourselves and build new capabilities.

We must invest in ourselves.
We must be willing to put our money where our mouth is. If we won't do it, then how can we expect others to do so? A prime example of this is having an emergency fund in place.

We must have a winning positive attitude.
There is nothing worse than a bad attitude. Author Keith Farrell says "the people who do best in life are those who realize they have the power to choose their attitudes, just as they have the power to choose their clothing, their cars, or their dinner companions."

We must have our own personal brand.
We must carve out a personal brand for ourselves, choosing not to depend solely on the brand of the companies we work for. Even if you have no aspirations of being an entrepreneur, a personal brand can serve you well inside the organization as you navigate corporate waters.

We must have a championship board (success squad) in place.
It is not enough to be our own champions. We must surround ourselves with people who are vested in our

successes. Of course, we retain the role as the captain of the team.

An example of an individual success squad includes:
- Oneself
- God
- Spouse/Significant Other
- Financial Planner
- Mentor
- Sponsor
- Coach
- Therapist
- Accountability Partner
- Cheerleader
- Babysitter/Nanny

An example of an entrepreneur success squad includes:

- Individual Success Squad (see above)
- Accountant
- Lawyer
- Business Coach/Advisor
- Business Development Manager
- Mastermind Group
- Virtual Assistant
- Therapist
- Insurance Agent
- Event Planner
- Copywriter

- Editor
- Graphic Designer
- And More

WAYS WE AVOID RESPONSIBILITY FOR OUR CAREERS

Having a *laissez faire* attitude about career ownership is a surefire way to avoid responsibility for one's career. Whether there is dependency on bosses, networks, or others, we often let people other than ourselves be the keepers of our fate. Our efforts match the fate keeper's when in reality, ours should far exceed them.

Some ways in which these manifest include:

Not being proactive
When we avoid actions that would drive results and wait for something to happen, we aren't being proactive.

Not tooting our horns
I'm reminded of a line from my daughter's favorite song, Wheels on the Bus: "*The horn on the bus goes beep beep beep…*" Are you saying beep beep beep when it comes to your career? I think most people aren't. As I think about the large network I have on LinkedIn, I think less than 50% are tooting their horns. Most people are busy focused on providing value, updates, or remaining silent.

We don't ask for what we want
This is a classic. Whether it is on the job or as a business owner asking for business, it is tough to ask for what you want. How tough is it to ask for a raise or promotion or to work flex time? These things are difficult because in our minds, we have created messaging that says we don't deserve it.

We aren't all in for networking
Networking is a skill that we all need in this day and age. We cannot get very far without leveraging the power of relationships.

And for some of us, we are still in denial. Examples include:
- We don't project a visually appealing image.
- We avoid or limit networking opportunities.
- We are scared of not providing enough value to our network, so we remain silent.
- We attend networking events, but upon reflection of the lack of connections made, we leave unsatisfied and unfulfilled, wondering if it was a good use of our time.
- We lack a plan around networking.
- We don't ask our network for what we need.

We have a bad attitude
Some folks are just on that train about how companies or bosses have wronged them. They get joy from resharing the story of how it's everyone else's fault. We are all human and I've definitely done my share of complaining about why it's not my fault. It can take eons to recognize your role in the

process. I think the key here is to acknowledge that stuff happens and that you're moving forward, not staying stuck in a forever case of the bad attitudes. It's time to move past the "woe is me" syndrome. Go get yours!

We are risk averse

There has to be a level of risk in place to promote greater successes. We have to risk in order to achieve greater gain. We have to risk failure to know and benefit from what's possible.

The great television writer Shonda Rimes says to embrace the yesses that come your way. Too often, we run the opposite way when opportunities come our way. They paralyze us with fear, giving us credence in the Impostor Syndrome which says, "I'm an impostor playing a role in my life."

We don't create a personal brand for ourselves

There are indeed some well-known, recognizable brands out there. General Motors, Kellogg's, Starbucks, Nike, Apple, Oprah, Huffington Post, and more. You get the gist. There is an opportunity for us to create our well-known brands. Now, I'm not suggesting that it has to be these billion-dollar brands, but there must be an awareness that you have a unique value proposition to offer and that you can in fact create a personal brand. In fact, you have a personal brand. What I'm trying to convey here is that you let others know about this personal brand and you take a role in steering the direction of said personal brand.

We don't take ownership

I do my job and I will get recognized and promoted. WRONG! If you're lucky, then it does work that way. But for the most part, you must take an active role in directing your career to where you want it to go.

We have to take ownership of moving from a place of waiting for change to happen. As Ghandi said, "Be the change you want to see."

We lack understanding of our environment

We are not aware of what's happening in our surroundings; the rules of engagement, if you will. In your environment, how do opportunities come about? Is it through job postings, networking, referrals? These are things you need to know and plan accordingly for. If you're bucking the environment by not understanding that the networking meetings are where it's happening, then it's a long road to get to where you desire to be.

We don't invest in our own development

These are indeed tough times and professional development is a "nice to have." Not so quick! There are many freebies available out there. It's a matter of whether we want to invest the time taking advantage of free training via universities (Coursera), YouTube and others willing to share their knowledge in exchange for your email address.

There are no sponsors on our team

Sponsors are a critical part of your success. They are the folks who believe in you and are willing to invest their dollars in your success. You've seen them all around. Think about the last time you attended a sporting event. Did you notice all the branding around you? What about events for causes? Have you noticed who's sponsoring the community outreach or support events? Yes, that's what we mean by sponsors. Sponsors believe in you and they go above and beyond to ensure your success. Lucky are the ones who realize the gem is having sponsors as a part of their strategies to powerfully own their careers.

There is no roadmap

Have you ever heard the phrase, "Proper planning prevents poor performance"? Well if you're counting on your mind as your roadmap, think again, for it is only one component of the solution. There must be a clearly outlined plan to meet your expected outcome. Hence, the high demand for project management.

We're afraid of failing

Failure is a rough one. It hurts like hell. But as the late Aaliyah said, "You have to dust yourself off and try again." Even better, Susan Jeffers said, "Feel the fear and do it anyway." You know what? They were both right.

We don't seek out opportunities

We don't seek out opportunities or make our own opportunities. That's that *laissez faire* (hands-off) behavior again. "An opportunity will find me if I just wait it out." Isn't that what we tell ourselves?

There is a mindset and acceptance required to take full ownership of your career. Otherwise, you will find yourself adrift, with many years past. You will be floating in a direction not entirely best suited to your happiness, though it may provide food and shelter, and if you're lucky, additional resources for travel and other luxuries.

Once upon a time, all I cared about was my compensation, my title, and my benefits. Did I have more than three weeks' vacation? SOLD! But there came a time where all those things weren't important. There was something missing inside. A knowing that I needed to create something that I could be proud of because it changed lives forever. You see, I wanted a career that allowed me to be a difference maker. It took many years out the gate for me to figure this out.

2 GAME-CHANGING CAREER BEHAVIORS

The way that we act is essential to successfully owning our career. We must carry ourselves in a professional manner. We must perform in a way that's demonstrative of creating a unique personal brand.

To "own" means there's a personal responsibility for the outcome of your career. There is a mindset and acceptance that *the results of my career has my hands all over it.* Personally, I can think of times when I did not take ownership of my career. I was never taught to. I had an expectation that if I stayed at my desk, minimized personal talk, and got my work done, it would be noticed, and as a result, I would move up the career ladder. When that didn't happen, I was puzzled. I observed others who were more social than I climbing the ladder. It was a frustrating time and it resulted in me becoming disillusioned. Perhaps you can relate to the feeling you get when your efforts aren't recognized or rewarded.

Here are some key behaviors to adopt in your quest to powerfully own your career:
- Ambitious: Demonstrating drive (action) necessary to achieve your goal.

- Articulate: Being able to speak your truth.
- Charming: Having finesse while delivering your message.
- Confident: Being clear that you are well able to deliver on what you go after.
- Courageous: Acting despite fear.
- Enthusiastic: Having a positive attitude.
- Flexible: Being open to change.
- Innovative: Being ideas-driven and being able to create.
- Productive: Being able to get the job done.
- Resilient: Being able to bounce back if things don't go your way.
- Risk-Appreciative: Open to taking opportunities that are out of your comfort zone.
- Trustworthy: Dependable

There are so many things you need to be in order to be successful. Most importantly, **you must be true to who you are at your core**. However, you have to take on some new behaviors to accelerate your success. You also have to acknowledge that you may have to act your way into being in some of these behaviors. Make a plan to upgrade your capabilities where there's a gap. There are many tools available to support your journey. In fact, I have discovered there are loads of free programs being offered. All that is required is your time commitment and willingness to do the work in order to reap the rewards.

3 HOW TO POWERFULLY OWN YOUR CAREER

To powerfully own your career, you must **DECIDE** and **CLAIM** that you want to sit in the driver's seat. You must know that you deserve better and be willing to not only do the requisite work, but be willing to go out on a limb to ensure your success.

Here are steps to powerfully own your career:

1. Take an audit of where you are in your career. An audit simply means taking the time to assess where you are in your career. Are you happy with your position? Are you happy with the company you work for? Are you happy working with the people you work with? Are you happy with your boss? Are you happy with the way you've been able to develop in your career? Are you happy with the promotion opportunities available to you in your career? Do you have a personal brand or is your brand non-existent and you are fine with the company brand defining your existence? There are many questions to consider when you take an audit. Document the answer to these questions and more. It may take you more than one sitting to complete this audit.

a) Sit on the information for a week or so. Allow yourself time to reflect to see if any additional thoughts arise and also the opportunity for what you've documented to resonate with you.

b) Decide what you want to keep the same and what you want to change. Tweak accordingly to get to a place that you feel comfortable using as a benchmark in the future.

2. Write out your goals to your place of a happy career. Create and write down affirmations to support those goals. Do not underestimate the power of affirming your desires. This will be fuel, especially if you aren't crystal clear on how you're going to achieve your goal.

3. Document the top-of-mind actions needed to accomplish those goals. Be gentle with yourself, knowing you don't have to have it all figured out and that you can revisit this step in the future.

4. Identify who you need to have involved to be successful. Who do you need on your success team?

5. Begin to form the necessary relationships. If you don't know the people you need, find ways to engage and build those relationships. Keep track of this so it doesn't get lost as this is a vital step in ensuring your success.

6. Up your online cache by leveraging LinkedIn to build your personal brand. LinkedIn is a wonderful social tool that facilitates making connections, building relationships, demonstrating thought leadership, and landing opportunities.

7. Fortify yourself. Keep your mind right with proper exercise, sleep, diet, resources, journaling, and more. Keep your mind in a positive place.

Powerfully owning your career means taking full responsibility for the career path you are seeking. With this ownership comes a willingness to get clear on the outcomes you are seeking, to define the support you require, and to create a plan to achieve your career goals. The best advice I can give to you is to be in tune with who you are in the process knowing that there will be challenges along the way. Test your feelings and know that if it doesn't feel good, you need to do something to get to a place where you're feeling good. You can stomp down the bad feelings, but they will eventually return, prompting action and results.

4 PLANNING YOUR CAREER

When I was going for my project management professional (PMP) certification, I created a plan and got sign-off from management. It entailed a list of the courses I needed to take and the support that I needed from management and the organization to be successful. I followed the plan to a tee and I was successful. The keys for success in that instance were:

1) I was clear on what I wanted, which was to gain a project management certification and to up my skills as a project manager.
2) I had a personalized plan that I was bought into, understanding that I was on the hook for doing the actions required to be successful.
3) I took persistent actions towards achieving my certification (training, exam preparatory course, and study time).
4) I tracked, measured, and tweaked my plan where necessary.
5) I sought input from others who had been successful before to ensure I had a solid plan.
6) I documented the support that I needed to be successful. Then I ASKED for it and I GOT it.
7) I celebrated the wins!

8) I created a repeatable process and mentored those behind me interested in the same goal.

Why do I share this story? I share it because most projects fail because not enough time is invested in the planning process. As you think about powerfully owning your career, a key step is investing the necessary time to create a solid plan. Additionally, a key input to the planning process is ensuring solid requirements are in place. You must be clear on what you are trying to accomplish. When you begin any new plan, it is helpful to spend some time <u>thinking</u> through where you are currently. I call that the stop-and-reflect moment. Life can cause us to move at a fast, reactionary pace without ample time for thinking through what we want and how we aim to get it.

What is your current situation and what about it do you want to change?

Next up is defining what you want to achieve. In my first book, *Achievement Unlocked: Strategies to Set Goals*, I emphasized the need to move from a place of vagueness to a place of specificity by answering the *what, when, where*, and *how* of your goals.

Examples of career-related requirements (goals) include:
- I would like a job that allows me the ability to work from home. (Remote working arrangements)

- I would like to work for someone who believes in me, is supportive of my development, and advocates for my abilities, resulting in promotions and greater leadership responsibility. (Mentor/Sponsor)
- I would like to have a senior leader (C-Suite) as my sponsor for leadership growth. (Sponsor)
- I would like an opportunity to leverage my talents in an international market. (Global opportunities)
- I would like to serve as a paid board member. (Board Role)
- I would like to secure an Executive MBA. (Higher Education)
- I would like to continue working in my current job with optimal performance and be able to retire with full pension at 55 years old. (Retirement Planning)
- I would like to be promoted at my company to a director-level position in the next two years. (Promotion)
- I would like to work on a diversified team that allows for my diverse perspectives to be listened to and acted upon. (Culture Fit)
- I would like the opportunity to engage with senior leaders on a regular basis. (Seat at the Table)

The biggest part of achieving your desires is being firmly rooted in the desire of being clear on what it is you want. Once you're clear on your true desires (requirements), you can move forward with identifying actions to achieve those desires.

Planning ahead of time can save you pain points on your journey to successfully achieving your goals. Anticipate that there will be some bumps in the road. When you encounter them, remember this wonderful quote from the late, great Maya Angelou.

"We may encounter many defeats but we must not be defeated."

Tips to Successfully Achieve Your Career Goals:
1. Follow the path of those before you who have successfully achieved what it is you desire to achieve. So, if Oprah is your *shero*, research her story and take heed of the wisdom and implement those that feel right to you.
2. Ask! In the midst of interviewing for this book, I found myself curious about the individuals I profiled. They had such intriguing stories, and I know that once you hit Chapter 7, you too will be inspired by their stories and their wisdom. I say "ask" because you can identify those around you who have the knowledge you seek. You just need the courage to ask for the support you need. It is indeed easier said than done, because for years I had access to leaders around me, but my pride and my mental mayhem told me that these potential mentors would not be accommodating in sharing their knowledge with me. I also didn't want to flag my shortcomings for fear that it would be used against me. Instead, I hopped along when there was an opportunity.
3. Spend! One of the greatest lessons I have learned is that I had power in my dollars. There was power to

cause movement; however, I was hesitant to touch my rainy-day fund and I found myself not committing to my true desires unless I was guaranteed a successful outcome. Again, that goes back to the mindset of not taking ownership of the outcomes I sought. I expected that my investment would work on its own. I believe in some cases it did. For example, once I secured my Master's degree, it was easier for me to jump in salary and switch companies than it had been previously. I think that experience caused me to believe it would continue to be that simple. It wasn't. I had to work hard and be strategic to create the upward movement I was seeking. When it didn't work as I had imagined, I became disillusioned. So, the moral of the story is to invest where you have gaps even if your company doesn't make the investment.

4. Turn rejection inside out. There is no doubt that you will be rejected in your quest. Some of those rejections may come as quite the shock. However, you can be successful. Like a boxer, you take the blow but you must get back up from the ground, regroup, and figure out your next move. Especially if you want to win. Arm yourself with evidence of others who have bounced back from rejection to greatness. Keep them in your line of sight as a motivating fuel to get you to build your resilience and to continue to be successful.

5. Find alliances that make sense for you. An example of this is if you're passionate about training, then the organization Association for Talent Development is a powerful organization to align yourself with. Likewise, if you're passionate about project management, then the true source to tap into is the Project Management Institute. There are countless organizations that align to whatever your goal is.

Leverage the organization as a support fuel to achieve your *how*.

6. Build a team of people to support you. The composition of your team may not necessarily be clear at the outset. However, as you gain insights and progress towards accomplishing your goals, the players become clearer. For me, as an entrepreneur, I became clearer on the team I needed when I participated in a mastermind group and got visibility from a successful leader. Some examples of who I needed for my *how* included an attorney, an insurance agent, an accountant, a bookkeeper, a webmaster, a virtual assistant, a graphic designer, etc. At the onset, I thought I could be successful with the bare bones, but as my competence grew, I gained clarity and courage to build the right team to help me achieve my goals.

5 PARTNERING WITH THE RIGHT PEOPLE

Oh, how important it is to your career to find the right people to connect with!

But how do you know who the right people are? Trust your gut! You know when you come across a gem. I have been fortunate to come across some wonderfully authentic, caring individuals in my career. I could tell because their actions told me so. When I needed an opportunity, they took my call and engaged me in conversation. They genuinely sought to help me succeed. I am forever grateful to those angels that God blessed me with.

Not surprisingly, I encountered people who didn't want to help me. Now, I know most of us are well intentioned. And as Don Miguel Ruiz advocated in *The Four Agreements*, you can't take it personally. Yes, Don, that is true, but it's also easier said than done. When you encounter those people, keep on your path. With every naysayer, there's a yes-sayer around the corner. That is what keeps you going. Relationships are key for career success.

Some key relationships that can shape your career include:

The Sponsor

For years, I was in the dark about the importance of having someone sponsor me in my career. "What's a sponsor?" I asked. "Someone who's willing to bet on your talents," I was told. "They believe in you and are willing to stand up for you and create opportunities when none exist." *Sounds good, but how do I get one, and who is the best person to play the role of a sponsor?* I thought.

I have to tell you that I found a sponsor when I wasn't looking for one. I wasn't looking because I didn't know I needed one.

A memorable sponsor appeared in my life when I really needed one. It began as a mentoring relationship and blossomed into a sponsorship (without the ask). He was encouraging and gave me wings to soar and demonstrate my capabilities.

#1 – He was kind. Sometimes we need someone to be kind to us when we are wounded.
#2 – He cast aside his title and gave me an ear to talk about my journey. He demonstrated genuine interest and asked me what I wanted. There's nothing like being asked what you want on the spot. I'm clear now on what I want but back then, I was a bit taken aback because I didn't really know what I wanted anymore. But, I opened my mouth and shared that I wanted to be happy. I wanted to make a difference. I wanted to be heard. I wanted a new path. I wanted an opportunity, even if I didn't have all the prerequisite skills

and I was rough around the edges. I wanted someone to invest in me because I was a darn good investment. The good news is, that was a game changing conversation and milestone in my career.

#3 – He took the information and did magic behind the scenes. The next thing I knew, I was working for him. Amazing, I know. I cannot tell you how blessed I felt to have that experience. Prepare yourself that things can happen pretty quickly with a sponsor in your corner.

#4 – He stayed connected with me for the season.

#5 – He gave me encouragement, like "Great job! Here's something for you to work on." He gave me leeway to demonstrate my leadership skills.

#6 – He allowed me to do reverse mentoring on him. That's right. I got to educate him from my vantage point.

I can keep going on. The point is, find yourself a sponsor. It doesn't have to be a senior executive, but someone who is willing to bat for you. They have influence that can be helpful on your journey and are willing to invest in you in terms of time, money, and more. If you can't find one in your organization, look outside and start building strategic relationships.

I will be forever grateful to him for what he did in my life. I'd like to think it was a win/win relationship as I was able to share my experiences as a black woman with him and he was able to share his experiences as a white male with me. We came from very different worlds but became friends. He was instrumental in setting me off on a new direction and chapter in my life. Thank you, Jeff.

partnership with. I believe that we can have multiple mentors for different facets of our careers as diverse individuals.

LinkedIn

Like the Johari Window Communications Model states, we have a blind spot. There are instances when we don't know what we don't know. So, I didn't know what I was missing out on and I daresay since I've since been enlightened.

I've come across many people who don't know the gem that they are missing with LinkedIn. An example of this is knowing the platform exists yet remaining hands off and instead fully embracing other social sites to remain just social. I was guilty of not spending time on LinkedIn. I have to believe that things happen in the time they are supposed to. Thankfully, I learned my lesson and am a regular user of the platform today. I can honestly say that I've gotten jobs and career offers via the platform that I did not apply for. These days we know that not all jobs are advertised. Therefore, we must be proactive in doing what we can to ensure we are in the driver's seat when it comes to our careers. And that means using LinkedIn.

LinkedIn can definitely be a valuable source for finding partners for your career success. It is common practice to look up individuals before you meet them. It is common practice to also ask a person if they are on LinkedIn in lieu of a business card. Even when I receive a business card, I still look for a person on LinkedIn so I can get a better understanding of commonalities to build a win/win relationship.

Associations

Did you know there is an Association of Master of Business Administration Executives? Leveraging the Directory of Associations, you can find associations for almost every interest. If there isn't, you're empowered to create one and bring together others wanting the same thing you're desiring. I think that's one of the reasons Meetups are so successful. Do a bit of research and find some relevant associations that you can use as a source for building more relationships in support of your career. When I switched over to Human Resources, I found out about the Society for Human Resources Management (SHRM). It was seen as a go-to place for HR professionals and so not only did I attend a meeting, I became a Board Member, and I volunteered to be a Diversity Director. It was really a great opportunity to further build my skills in a new function and develop new relationships that would later impact my career.

Conferences

Attend not just from an education standpoint, but from a position of building relationships and getting your voice heard. This may mean volunteering to be a part of a planning committee or being a speaker, panelist, or blogger for the conference. If your company won't invest the dollars because they can't see the ROI, think long and hard about your goals and determine whether you're worth the investment. Hint: If you won't invest in yourself, why should your company? Partners are waiting for you in this space.

Other Networking Opportunities

The world is your oyster. Go forth, and as Shonda Rimes says, say yes to experiences waiting to educate you. Get strategic about your networking. Where do you need to be? Who do you need to talk to? Read the networking books. Assess the event you're thinking of attending. What can you gain from it? Do you have pre-work or post-work to do?

Today is a good day to think about the partnerships that you have in place and the opportunities you have to build new partnerships to help you succeed in your career. For the most part, people are willing to help you. Be clear on what it is you are asking for. Are you asking for a mentor? Are you asking for sponsorship? Are you asking for introductions? Whatever your ask, be clear in your mind before setting out to make it a reality.

6 PROMOTING YOUR CAREER

Promoting is about being in tune with your personal brand.

Does Your Personal Brand Exist?
Do people know who you are and what you can deliver?
- We know the brand Starbucks and that it delivers a space for connecting over delicious coffee.
- We know Google as an online search engine that we can ask any question.
- We know Amazon as an online retailer that saves us time by offering everything we can think of and we can practically get it all in two days.
- We know we can get our favorite television show on Hulu or Netflix.

What is your brand? Do you feel comfortable sharing your brand?
Let's be clear: we all have a brand. Some are more known than others. That is because there is a comfort level with promoting the brand. Whether it is done by the individual themselves or a spokesperson, the brand must be promoted. People need to know what your brand represents so they can seek out your brand and support your brand.

When you enter a networking event, do you confidently lead with the name of the company that you're working for or do you lead with your personal brand?

There's a certain amount of cache that more well-known brands have and so it goes without saying that there is a comfort level behind a proven brand. The opportunity for the individual lies with focusing on building out their personal brand. Opportunities are there for the taking. One must be brave and known in their hearts that all brands start somewhere and then grow and that's what you have to do with your personal brand.

Can others vouch for your brand?

There is an untapped community who have had a sample and are willing to vouch for the quality of your brand as one that is worthy of being supported. The power of social influence allows others to provide recommendations, reviews, and sharing of our personal brands. We must do the work necessary to provide a continuing flow of support for our personal brands.

Marianne Williamson, author of *A Return to Love: Reflections on the Principles of "A Course in Miracles"* said, **"There is nothing enlightened about shrinking so that other people won't feel insecure around you. We are all meant to shine . . ."**

Keep that message somewhere close so that you can remind yourself that you need to shine. Shining = promoting your career.

Bravely share with the world that you're here! **I'm here.**

Communicate

Let your voice be heard. Some of us may have trouble doing so because of our cultural upbringing but these days, speaking up is a good thing to do. Now, I'm not saying you can't have allies who speak on your behalf. Nor am I saying that you need to be untrue to your introversion preference. The key is continuing to gain strategies to elevate your career to the place of your choosing.

If you're afraid of speaking publicly, find a Toastmasters club and build up your communications skills. A lot of companies offer internal Toastmasters clubs. I was privileged to be a part of the Toastmasters community for a number of years. I've also been a coach to organizations with internal Toastmasters clubs. I'm always surprised that the numbers aren't staggering, especially since in most cases companies were covering the cost of membership and all that was required was time and effort.

I recommend finding opportunities to communicate. If within your position, you're not getting an opportunity to communicate the way you envision, find opportunities for your voice to be heard. In my case, being an advocate for the diversity & inclusion agenda gave me leadership opportunities.

Release

Release any negative baggage that you're carrying around with regard to your career. Some examples may include having a Bad Boss who impacted your self-confidence. Perhaps you had a bad performance review that you just can't shake. Maybe you have a bad attitude because your company isn't recognizing your talents with a promotion. Whatever it is, you need to shake it off. Pour into yourself until you're healed. That means educating yourself, finding a source of joy by engaging with others on a similar journey, finding a mentor and sponsor, reaffirming yourself with positive language, and seeking out opportunities that give you the experiences you need to succeed.

Ask

Ask for what you want. Plain and simple. The Bible says, "Ask and ye shall receive." It's that simple, but it can be scary because no's can hurt like heck. We have to do the work to gain our confidence to ask for things. Keep a log of asks and the associated responses. Then glean insights from what you have learned along the way to help you continue to ask for what you need to be successful.

So often we take what we get even if we're not satisfied. We may not want to get hurt or to hurt someone by our ask and so we limp along with what we have. This is indeed not a recipe for success. And so, we must find the courage to dare to ask for what we need. If needed, invest in educating yourself in the art of negotiation. Remember everyone didn't start out the gate being super sophisticated with getting whatever they desired. Our exposures feed into our way of being and our perspectives are formed in that manner.

Tools to Support the Promote Process:

Updated Resume — A resume is the traditional useful tool that captures the *where* and *what* you've done in your career. How many of us in our careers have ensured that document is up to date when we aren't looking for a job? Then once we determine its time to move on, we're scrambling to create updated resumes. Yes, it's worth it to pay the resume writer. You will surely save yourself time in addition to building your confidence when you see the quantifiable benefits in black and white that you've accomplished along the way.

Biography Statement — A one-pager on your background in a story form is useful to have. Should you decide to speak or be a panelist, this biography will prove useful for you to have ready.

Networking Brief — This document came to my attention while attending a class at an outplacement firm. Often times when you are networking, the receiver isn't sure of how they can help you. The networking brief is a one-page document outlining a summary of who you are, what you're looking for, and how the person you're networking with can help you. This indeed was a valuable takeaway for me and I've proved its usefulness in countless networking meetings where the person I was networking with was grateful to have some direction on how they could be of assistance. The brief does not replace your resume.

Row 1 – Clyde Tinnen, Deb Dagit, David L. Kim, Malaika Myers
Row 2 – Nancy Di Dia, Joseph Santana, Havilah Malone, Marc Stephenson Strachan
Row 3 – John Lahey, Tomiko Fraser-Hines, Eric Pliner, Mohammed Murad
Row 4 – Laura Skandera Trombley, Harry Rilling

7 LEADERSHIP PROFILES

In this chapter, I will highlight the diverse candidates I've interviewed and allow you the opportunity to meet them through the sharing of their stories in their own words.

Those interviewed are a cross-selection of different genders, ethnicity, sexual orientation, and abilities across various industries. In addition, they bring to the conversation diverse perspectives and leadership styles.

Name	Perspective	Industry
Clyde Tinnen	Black Male	Legal
Deb Dagit	Disabled White Female	Consulting
David L. Kim	Asian Male	Entrepreneur
Malaika Myers	Black Female	Hospitality
Nancy Di Dia	Gay White Female	Pharmaceuticals
Joseph Santana	Hispanic Male	Entrepreneur
Havilah Malone	Black Female	Entrepreneur
Marc Stephenson Strachan	Black Male	Marketing
John Lahey	White Male	Higher Education
Tomiko Fraser-Hines	Black Female	Modeling
Eric Pliner	Gay White Male	Consulting
Mohammed Murad	Asian Male	Entrepreneur

Name	Perspective	Industry
Laura Skandera Trombley	White Female	Higher Education
Harry Rilling	White Male	Government

Clyde Tinnen
Partner
Withers Bergman LLP

I met Clyde in the Urban League Leadership Development Program in Stamford, Connecticut. The program was designed to provide advanced leadership training that could be applied to impactful community service. I remember being impressed by his character and easy-going nature. We struck up a friendship that's lasted over two decades. He has an excellent legal mind and I count on him as a true advisor. Here is his inspiring story.

The Story

I was born and raised in Norwalk, CT. I did my undergrad at William & Mary. Unfortunately, I did not apply myself while I was there and did not make very good grades. I applied to law school as a senior and was flatly rejected by the two schools that I applied to: Quinnipiac and The University of Bridgeport.

I worked in non-profits for a few years and then made a move into the for-profit sector with my first job being at Quad Graphics in Wisconsin. I worked there for two years before I was recruited away to Quebecor World in North Haven, CT. I had lots of different roles at Quebecor World, starting in customer service before doing stints in sales, finance, and accounting. I earned my MBA in Finance at University of Connecticut during this time. About one year after earning my MBA, I became a father for the first time. Being a dad inspired me to apply to law school again, this time fortunately with a stellar business school record behind me. I was accepted to law school and started on my son's first birthday.

I graduated from law school at Columbia University in 2006. After graduating, I worked for three and a half years at the top-rated law firm in the world, Cravath, Swaine & Moore LLP. I then took my talents to Kelley, Drye & Warren LLP, where I became a partner in 2014. I moved my practice and became a partner at Withers Bergman LLP in 2015, where I continue to practice.

Owning Your Career

Ownership of one's career is liberating from the standpoint that retaining the ultimate responsibility and terms of what is acceptable (or not) for one's own career is much more empowering than passively approaching one's career as a participant, where everyone else (your boss, your spouse, your friends, etc.) dictates the rules of the game, the score and players.

How Taking Risks Impacted Clyde's Career Journey

Taking risks has been important. I began my law school career in an evening program so that I could maintain full-time employment during the day. I was married, owned my own home and was the father of a one-year-old when I began law school, so I did not think that I had a real choice as to whether I had to work or not. After excelling in the classroom during my first year, I decided to apply to transfer to a more prestigious full-time day program. Going to law school full time meant that I would lose out on my full-time income, but it also meant that I would complete law school earlier with more job opportunities. After much deliberation, I decided that the risk of leaving my full-time employment was worth it. I betted on myself and I made the right decision.

Avoidance

Early in my career, I was identified as an up-and-coming star within a firm that I used to work for. I was selected for a program where I attended leadership training and met many people in senior leadership. I was also interviewed for senior positions in the country. One such position was a senior human resources position as a global lead of executive compensation. I was offered the role, which was to be based in Montreal. Despite the firm's confidence in my abilities and desire to promote me, I lacked the confidence to accept this role in an area of the company that I had no experience in. I also had some trepidation about moving out of the U.S. Unfortunately, I declined the role and still regret not taking that shot.

The Formula for Owning Your Career

I think the formula for owning one's career is something that I picked up from Zig Ziglar. His approach for winning in life is called the "will, skill, and refill" approach. Basically, summoning the desire, effort, and attitude to seek out success, however one defines it — the will. Learning and developing the tools and planning to achieve one's objectives — the skill. Finally, committing to lifelong learning, work-life balance and sustainable outcomes — the refill. Mr. Ziglar's famous approach for a successful life also applies to careers.

Key Relationships

My family (including me) have been most responsible for my success. My parents shaped my world outlook and values but also gave me the great gift of exceptionally high expectations. My own family (my wife and my three sons) have also inspired me to be my best. I'm told that we only retain small percentages of what we read or hear but retain up to 90% of things that we teach to others. Trying to be a good example and teaching my boys things has taught me volumes about life. My wife has also inspired me and challenged me to collaborate and build something bigger together than anything we could have built on our own.

Mentoring and Sponsorships as Career Levers

Mentors and sponsors greatly enhance one's likelihood of success and if one is available, I always encourage everyone to seek them out. However, the lack of a mentor or sponsor is not a disqualifier for success. Admiring role models from afar can also be impactful and help one visualize what success might look like. I was fortunate to have a great professional mentor who made my success personal (to him). He also taught me a lot of the day-to-day qualities and personality traits that I believe have been instrumental in my career success.

Sharing Career Successes

I seek out others who are peers or more junior colleagues who seem open to input and offer my feedback.

Career Advice

- Treat your career like it is a free-standing business.

The Mentor

Mentoring is a powerful alliance. The idea that you can tap someone who's gone before you and been successful to pour their knowledge into you to help you succeed is just wonderful.

Over my career, I've had formal and informal mentors. Formal mentors were assigned in organizations that I've worked with. In a structured formal process, senior leaders can be identified and paired with junior talent to impart their knowledge. Informally, I've experienced mentorship without putting a label on it. Those are the people who are kind enough to share their knowledge without any outcome attached to it.

If you don't have a mentor (formal or informal), it's a worthwhile investment of time. It can be daunting to ask for the help you need, but keep in mind that hearing "no" won't kill you. In fact, I heard someone say at a conference that it was wise to shift your perspective of a no to "next opportunity." That's valuable advice, I'd say.

If the person you want to mentor you is too tied up to take on the role, then find another person or get creative on how you can still have a mentoring relationship. This could mean being flexible on frequency or mode of communication. The point that I want to impart to you is that you can define the structure of the alliance you want to have with your mentor. And you get to decide who you will engage in a mentoring

- Define what you have to offer to the world narrowly enough so that it is relevant to your "market" but not so narrowly that you cannot be flexible and pivot when new opportunities present themselves outside of your comfort zone.

Deb Dagit
Entrepreneur/Consultant
Deb Dagit Diversity LLC

Deb Dagit was born with a brittle bones condition (Osteogenesis Imperfecta) that resulted in her experiencing at least 70 broken bones and over 30 major surgeries. She has not just survived but thrived, and continues to have a very successful career as an advocate, corporate executive leader, and entrepreneur. I'm pleased to include her story in *The Power of Owning Your Career*. Truly, there are valuable nuggets at every turn.

The Story

When I was in college, I started out as pre-med, but because I had missed a lot of math and science due to being treated for brittle bones when I was a kid, I quickly learned that was not an option. The tutors I had worked with in middle and high school were good about the other subjects, but for some reason none of them were very good about helping me keep up with math and science. So, I switched over to Clinical Psychology and that was what my undergrad and graduate degrees were in.

The dean of the school during my Master's program said that I needed to choose a career that was research oriented because as a person with a visible disability (I am short-statured at 4'2") I wouldn't be successful in securing clients. This was eye-opening feedback because at the time I was getting really good grades, and at that age it hadn't occurred

61

to me that people wouldn't take me seriously or trust me as a psychotherapist because of how I looked.

This experience with applied psychology caused me to realize that what I really wanted to do was use what I was learning in a workplace setting. At that time, Industrial and Organizational Psychology was just beginning to be offered as others were coming to similar realizations. At that same company, where I worked for about four years, I regularly applied for promotional opportunities but they wouldn't even interview me. People as high as the head of Human Resources told me unabashedly, "We're not going to interview you. Don't bother applying. You know, you're lucky to have a job." This wasn't like ancient history. This was in the mid-'80s. Fortunately, a law called COBRA took effect in 1987 that allowed you to keep your medical benefits even if you quit your job. With a pre-existing condition, I could not be without health benefits. I quit that dead-end job and started a non-profit organization that I ran for four years called Bridge to Jobs. Because our approach was so innovative, we were recognized as a successful new community of practice model for accelerating job placement of people with a broad range of disabilities that others began to replicate.

This new approach also caught the attention of lots of well-connected people. We even ended up in the Smithsonian. Most memorably my Congressman, Norm Mineta, who was a key co-sponsor of a new piece of civil rights legislation called The Americans with Disabilities Act, reached out to me. He asked me to fly to Washington, DC to address concerns that his colleagues on Capitol Hill had about the

THE POWER OF OWNING YOUR CAREER

ADA. We were able to combat fear with facts, and the ADA finally passed. Congressman Mineta invited me to be at the signing ceremony on the South Lawn of the White House. As I flew home from that momentous occasion, I decided it was time to go back into the corporate world where I thought I could have the greatest impact. I went from being an administrative-level HR person at a semiconductor company, to running a small non-profit, to becoming an entry-level executive at a big and very fast-growing tech company in a little less than five years.

Owning Your Career

By redoubling my efforts when people told me I couldn't do something. By standing up for myself and what I believe. Quitting a job that wasn't right for me and creating my own opportunity through a non-profit, helping to define the field of diversity and inclusion, and creating a consulting practice to mentor and support other D&I practitioners.

How Taking Risks Impacted Deb's Career Journey

Life is a risk every time I get in a car. I could become seriously injured or even killed by a fender-bender. I guess it's all relative. What might have seemed to others to be big risks: leaving a job when COBRA was available, threatening to sue the Governor of the State of California, making decisions outside the scope of a contractor role...all those could have backfired, and I could have been without a job. I come from working-class roots. I didn't have a backup plan. I didn't have parents who were going to help me. I was living on my own. I had a strong sense of purpose and followed my heart and passion for social justice. I think the bigger risk would have been to internalize the low expectations others had and stay in a dead-end job feeling bored and frustrated.

Avoiding Responsibility for One's Career

One of the things I never want to do again that I was terrible at was performance management, especially when someone wasn't performing well. That's deadly because it hurts the whole team if you let someone slide who isn't doing what they're supposed to do.

There was a time when I had two employees who were from an underrepresented group and who were not meeting their job expectations and it was affecting my team. I was initially scared to do what I needed to because they were extremely well networked in the company, and they had already made it clear that they would accuse me of discrimination if I did anything about their performance issues. Even the legal department at the company warned me about putting them on a performance improvement plan.

It took me longer than it should have. I did do the right thing, and I had to get the help of the General Counsel because I knew that the employee relations department and HR and the employee resource groups were all going to take me to task when I did this no matter what the circumstances were. When you manage performance issues it is confidential, even if you wanted to make your case, your hands are tied, you can't explain what is going on.

I regret that I didn't do more sooner because I think it caused everyone to suffer and it wasn't very brave on my part to take so long. Today, I enjoy developing and mentoring others but would just as soon be a solopreneur versus having to manage anyone else's performance.

The Formula for Owning Your Career

I think that, first of all, when you reach a plateau, especially if you're getting bored, then you need to set a new goal. You need to tell yourself not to stay comfortable, and to try something new. If I'd have stayed in Silicon Valley, it would have been so much easier. I called it the foothills of diversity and inclusion because if you live in California, diversity and inclusion is the milieu that you're in. It's all around you in the neighborhood, in the school, in the grocery store.

Key Relationships

Merck's CEO Richard T. Clark. Dick and I forged a strong bond. He was my sponsor and champion in so many ways. He insisted that I be promoted to a higher level of executive, that I get more resources, and that I present more regularly to the Board. He teased when he spoke to our Employee Resource Groups that he reported to me. I had some very challenging situations within the HR function where my role sat, which by the way, is not at all unusual for a diversity leader, and he was always in my corner. Ken Frazier was also a great sponsor. He helped convince me to join Merck when he was the General Counsel and was always helpful when I needed support or advice. I knew he would become the CEO one day and was so happy I got to see him take on that role.

I nurtured these and other relationships with mentors and sponsors by taking every opportunity to return the favor by making them look good in ways and places that mattered to them, and preparing them well when they needed to visibly stand up for diversity and inclusion under difficult circumstances.

Mentoring and Sponsorships as Career Levers

I was incredibly fortunate to have the benefit of a lot of amazing mentors and sponsors within the diversity and inclusion field who helped accelerate my learning and give me honest feedback. One of those, Ted Childs, encouraged me to look at jobs out on the East Coast. I don't think I would have had the courage or emotional stamina to take on such a big change and challenge if not for wise and supportive leaders like Ted, Claudette Whiting at DuPont, Gene Andrews at GE, Jose Berrios at Gannett, Dr. Johnnetta B. Cole on the Merck Board, and several others who always returned my calls and e-mails with encouragement and confidence in my ability when I felt overwhelmed or confused.

I think that each person takes you where you need to go in your journey at the time. When I was at the semiconductor company where I couldn't get a promotion, the head of EEO and affirmative action, Judee Williams, taught me the basics around employment law and statistics and knowing how to write up a compliant Affirmative Action plan. She was also a friend to me and got me out of a bad situation where I was being blatantly discriminated against by my client group. I need to say that most of my mentors and sponsors have been African American men and women. I did not find other people with disabilities in any role to be a sponsor, at least anybody who owned their disability (75% of disabilities are non-apparent). I also had a few LGBTQ sponsors.

I've been very fortunate. But I also have to say that like anybody who's had a long career, there have also been very senior people who didn't treat me well, who openly bullied me. Those are folks you learn from too. You learn to find your truth. You learn how to speak up. You learn how to stand up, not only for yourself, but for others feeling vulnerable. You learn how to do the right thing under difficult, high-conflict circumstances.

Sharing Career Successes

I mentor a lot of people, both formally and informally. I mentor just about anyone who asks me for help. Many young people who are in college or are early career professionals find me and I am happy to make time for them and encourage and inform the path they want to follow.

In my consulting practice I mentor my clients, many of whom are learning this trade and are needing some support along the way. I'm not on the speaking circuit, but I do sometimes share information via keynotes, training sessions, webinars and then other types of presentations that people can record and replay.

Self-promotion can be a big challenge that many women face. I don't see very many men who have that problem, but most women tend to believe your actions ought to speak for themselves. When you start a consulting business though, if you are reluctant to toot your own horn, you're going to be in trouble because you have to demonstrate your skills and experience in order to win business. You have to effectively share what you're capable of delivering.

Valuable Online Tools for Career Management
Having a website, contributing to discussions on Facebook, Twitter and LinkedIn, and consuming information from trusted online sources like the Harvard Business Review and Fast Company, are all very helpful. Being a part of the dialogue keeps me current, burnishes my personal brand as a D&I consultant, and helps me stay connected with colleagues and friends I rarely get to see in person.

Career Advice
When you're younger, you think that the way you're going to find your one true love, your great career choice, or any other aspiration, is that it is just going to fall into your lap if you are a good person. Even if you don't think opportunities will just magically manifest, you may at least wish that's the way it was and be more than a little afraid to walk out the door and go find what you want.

Successfully owning and excelling in your career is similar in many ways to dating. You have to have high standards, not give yourself away (equal pay for equal work), and often try things you're not sure you will be good at. You must be committed to not settling for a job until you find a work environment and job role that is aligned to your purpose, passion, and potential, and then you have to work like hell to nail it.

You have to try new things. You have to learn a lot about the company that you work for, decide whether you genuinely like or maybe even love it, and if what they do and how they do it is in integrity with your values. If there is alignment, your career has great potential as you can clearly see how you will contribute to their mission. On the other hand, if there's something about the culture that's toxic, it's like a bad boyfriend. Get out of there. Don't stay in a bad work relationship out of fear you will not find something better. You have to have the courage and patience to hold out for the right match.

I would encourage people to consider reading two of Malcolm Gladwell's books, *Outliers* and *Blink*. Not because like they are great scientific treatises, but because there are a lot of valuable self-insights that will serve your career.

For the early career professional, become an outlier: There's a lot of great advice offered as to what you need to do if you want to go from being good at your job to being truly great. Blink is helpful for people who have been in their career for a long time and need to remember that it's okay to trust themselves to make good choices and take innovative risks, even if most people disagree with you!

One other resource I would suggest is Sylvia Ann Hewlett's book *Executive Presence*. So many people who want to grow their career and are on the cusp of becoming an executive-level leader are told they don't have sufficient executive presence. There is nothing more annoying than getting that feedback because it is rarely defined and may sound like you have to somehow change your personality or other aspects of what makes you, you. Sylvia does a great job of unpacking what is meant by the term "executive presence" and explains how you can live in integrity with who you are, be your own person, and still be recognized as having that elusive quality that can make or break your career.

David L. Kim
Founder/CEO
IAMBIC Group LLC

I had the pleasure of meeting David during my tenure at Diageo. He was a part of the Diageo Multicultural Marketing Advisory Group (DMMAG). I had exposure to the group because of my role in leading the African Heritage Employees at Diageo. I jokingly think of David as an E.F. Hutton. That means, when he speaks, you listen. He was always very nice to me, genuinely listened to me, and made me feel welcome. When you have those experiences, you don't forget them wherever you go.

So, it goes without saying that I stayed in touch with David after my time at Diageo ended. He is someone to be admired and to learn from. It was a no-brainer for me to include him in *The Power of Owning Your Career*.

I know with certainty that you'll enjoy his story and pick up some valuable, inspirational knowledge along the way.

The Story
I am a first-generation American of Korean descent. My parents immigrated to the United States in the mid-'50s, after the Korean War. I was born in New Jersey and grew up in the US.

Over my career, I have had the good fortune of gaining experience in the media, corporate, government, and nonprofit sectors, domestically and internationally.

I was the inaugural editor of the Asian American Journalists Association (AAJA) convention newspaper, called The Daily AAJenda. This was in 1990. And it was a fun project. It was the first time that any minority journalist association desktop-published the convention newspaper.

It was a great management experience. I picked the editorial staff, production team and I oversaw several section editors and layout editors, as well as set up the daily editorial briefing and assignment meetings. And ultimately, I was responsible for making sure the paper not only was delivered, but that the quality of the paper was beyond reproach. It was an incredibly exhausting week, which could have been a nightmare if I hadn't picked the right people, get them all on the same page, and inspire them to do whatever it took to get the job done. Clarity of purpose, responsibilities, and expectations had to come from me. Without alignment and understanding, no matter how great the people were, this would not have been a success.

One of the AAJA convention attendees I met was a corporate relations manager from Anheuser Busch. We exchanged pleasantries but it was more a chance meeting than anything else. The next thing I knew, I was asked to consider being interviewed for a position with Anheuser Busch. And this was interesting, because up until that time, I was pretty much on an academically oriented career path.

I had already interviewed and accepted a job at the Asia Society to head the Korean Affairs desk. When the call came from Anheuser Busch, in the space of a week I got plane tickets, flew out, had my job interview, and received a job offer on the Friday before the Monday I was supposed to start my new job. That was a little bit awkward.

I accepted the Anheuser-Busch job and apologized profusely to the Asia Society. The person who hired me actually became a really good friend of mine. And I returned the favor to him by speaking at one of his conferences in Chicago, years later, free. I owed him a favor and he was gracious to allow me to repay the favor in that regard.

I thought I had burned a bridge, but handling the situation the way that I did allowed me to not only keep my reputation intact, but also by not forgetting the kindnesses shown to me, I was able to turn a potential negative into a positive that still exists today.

The first part of my career with Anheuser Busch, where I spent nearly 15 years, started out in New York City, and then a year after I started, in St. Louis where their corporate headquarters are located.

That's where I gained a significant part of my formative education, if you will, business education: working for a large corporation, getting a sense of what I was good at, the importance of establishing relationships, having an impact, and knowing the difference between output and outcomes.

Another key learning was understanding how to succeed in a matrixed environment and the value of creating and exercising virtual influence and management. Taking that experience and applying it to the positions I had later on was very helpful. After Anheuser Busch, I received an appointment to become the Chief of Staff at the United States Mint. That was my first foray into the C-suite. It was a very interesting situation, because the director of the United States Mint was of Chinese descent.

This was the first time that I directly reported to another Asian. I enjoyed my experience there, though it was crazy at times. I gained valuable insights into how the federal government works, and at times, doesn't work. I absolutely appreciated the opportunity to serve our country. Also, it is interesting to note that prior to my time at the U.S. Mint, I had only reported to African Americans and Latinos.

Following that, I joined for a short time a boutique public affairs firm called The Raben Group. Then I was with AARP to start their Asian American marketing and outreach department.

After I successfully started that department, I had an opportunity to go into consulting, which was really kind of fun for me to do, because it gave me the ultimate freedom of picking who I wanted to work with, and picking the projects that I wanted to work on. Luckily, during the early part of my career, I was able to establish a financial foundation that gave me more freedom to consider all my options.

I think it's important for young people to understand the importance of a financial foundation. In other words, it's one thing to job hop for a higher salary, but if you don't accumulate some basic wealth in terms of pension/401K, etc., it becomes a constraint later on in life.

Owning Your Career

I was fortunate to be given certain opportunities early on in my career, for example, I gave the department presentation to the president-CEO of the company within the first year of being hired at Anheuser-Busch. That could have been a career-ender. I had to memorize a 45-slide deck and had over 400 backup slides in binders. I was put to the test, and obviously, I passed. But I was the lowest-ranking person to give a department presentation. Everybody else was a vice president or higher. I was only a director at the time, in front of the CEO with 30 of the top execs. So, preparation for those opportunities was paramount. It's one of those things where you never know when it's going to happen. When those things happen, you have just got to hit it out of the ballpark.

Presentation skills need to be polished and one has to be a compelling speaker. Because that's what levels the playing field for minorities. If you are an exceptional speaker, people take notice because despite what they see, when they hear your voice, this makes a difference and often overcomes a lot of stereotypical questions and doubts. That was my takeaway.

How Taking Risks Impacted David's Career Journey

The old cliché of taking risks is obviously important, but it's also measuring the risk and knowing what the upside and downside is. More importantly, know who's in your corner when you decide to take a risk. For me, there have been calculated risks and missed opportunities, no doubt. That said, I think it relates to understanding the culture and the environment that you're in, because you have to first understand what the appetite for risk is. And, quite honestly, at Anheuser-Busch and in the beer industry, there was a significant amount of appetite for risk. I believe that risks taken by minorities in corporations are seen and handled differently than in government or at a non-profit.

But know that if you do take the risk, you have to deliver. Because then when you ask for forgiveness, it is a lot easier to get that rather than, as they say, the opposite, where you ask for permission and they don't understand or they don't believe. There are some times when you have to take a risk, make it happen, and then when you apologize, they say, "Hey, it was okay."

Avoiding Responsibility for One's Career

Being the oldest in my family and part of more than just several consecutive generations of "oldest and first sons," I've often wondered if responsibility has become part of my DNA. I can't say that I've ever "avoided" responsibility, certainly not in the typical "that's not might fault" sort of way. And indeed, there were some uncomfortable times for taking the heat."

The Formula for Owning Your Career

I don't know if there's a one formula that works, but let me suggest what my takeaways are. Number one, it's the depth and quality of the relationships that you develop. I had to develop a significant amount of trust for Anheuser Busch to peel off a million bucks in their budget for me, but I delivered on outcomes that made others look good. I didn't have to take credit. I gave them full credit, but you do that enough, and people understand that there is someone behind the scenes making this happen.

Secondly, education. Helping those folks understand that the multicultural business opportunities, whether it's through outreach or marketing, is not an either/or proposition. And let's face it, America is changing. Demographics are changing, and for corporations, they're less concerned about the color of the person who buys the beer as long as the beer is being sold. They look for expertise. They look for the best way to do this.

Key Relationships

Growing up on the East Coast, as opposed to most Koreans, who grew up on the West coast or Korea, was a different experience for me. Also, both my parents were professionals. That had a lot to do with forming my outlook on what it means to be bi-cultural. The immigrant experience varies, as you can imagine, across the board depending upon different ethnicities and races. As American citizens of Korean descent, my parents afforded me the opportunity to grow up learning how to appreciate being an American of Korean descent.

Mentoring and Sponsorships as Career Levers

I had some challenges where some of the Latinos who I supervised wanted to go around me and go directly to the VP, who was also Latino. He and I had a great relationship and he pushed back on these people and said, "Deal with David first, don't come to me, he's your supervisor and if you have an issue or something you go him, don't come to me because I happen to be Latino. Don't disrespect the chain of command." I owe a lot to him, in part because he understood that loyalty can motivate great performance almost as much as lack of management insecurity.

Having the right mentor/sponsor is critical because there are challenges even within multicultural departments and multicultural situations, since you throw all the different sorts of multicultural groups together. But having someone who had my back, having the type of quality relationship that I had with someone of a different ethnicity, different race, and the trust level was huge to my success, and in turn allowed me to create successes for him. Until I got the job at the Mint, most of my bosses or sponsors were not Asian; they were either African American or Latino, and in some cases, white, but up until that time, I'd never had an Asian boss.

Sharing Career Successes

I was fortunate to learn early in my career that success often depends upon developing the type of relationships where you work on projects together and understand that making someone else win or look good will allow you to still reap the accolades later on. It's not a matter of, "I have to show that I'm successful." Making one's boss look good goes without saying. But helping even peers, people that you don't necessarily report to, creates that 360 sound chamber, where your name comes up more often from different places. That's how you achieve greater success. Your boss is not just telling his boss how great you are; it's other people from other departments who may be as influential or even more influential in different way.

Valuable Online Tools for Career Management

Far too often the internet or texting has become a substitute for effective communication. Especially among the younger folks. I can't stress enough how important it is to avoid misunderstanding to get a better and deeper level of true understanding through face to face. That's first choice. Second obviously is phone call. But I think it would be huge mistake to become so overly reliant on text messages and emails, especially because it's not in real time.

Career Advice

It's more effective and more important if someone else toots your horn. Create your own situations. In the course of the presentations I mentioned earlier, I showed senior management a couple of interesting things. Number one, Anheuser-Busch is a global beer company, but they weren't really paying attention to some of the marketing opportunities that existed between Asia and the U.S.

What I wanted to show them was the importance of having a global Asian marketing program, or strategy, that says, "Look, Asians have culturally and experientially driven consumer purchasing behavior regardless of whether they're living in Asia or United States. For example, we can achieve some scale of economy if you launch a Lunar New Year ad that could be run not only in the U.S., but in any country where there are Asians."

Often thinking out of the box does not produce immediate buy-in, but the point is to never give up, especially if this is something within your area of expertise. Someday, someone will take note and things will happen. It's never a question of if, but when.

Malaika Myers
Chief Human Resource Officer
Hyatt International

I met Malaika at a National Black MBA Chapter meeting in New York. It was a case of networking gone right, which resulted in a friendship. We stayed connected over the years and to my surprise, we ended up working for the same company. Malaika clearly was rocking the house with her skills because she came into the organization and very quickly moved up the ranks of senior leadership in the human resources organization. She worked globally and these days is calling the shots over at Hyatt with a very large employee base. Malaika is super humble but a force to be reckoned with. I admire her talent and was grateful she agreed to allow me to include her as a profile for *The Power of Owning Your Career.*

The Story
My career has spanned from Pepsi, to Diageo, to Arysta, to Jardin, to Hyatt. I started at FMC Chemical Company in a plant in North Tonawanda, New York. I then went on to Princeton, NJ, then Pepsi in Texas, California, and then New York. That was the first 10 years. Next, I was promoted to the vice president level. I planned to be there for another 10 years, but I decided I wanted to move somewhere else and be successful. That's where Diageo came in.

At Diageo, I had both babies and I took five months off. When I had my son Evan, I talked to my boss so I could go back just four days per week. I worked that schedule for two and a half years. I read every Friday in preschool. I had flexibility and yet it didn't impact my career. The Arysta CEO respected other parts of my life as well as my skills. You are empowered to make it work for you. I decided on the role I wanted to do before I retire. That's the part I took real ownership in. No one's thinking about your career as much as you are! It wasn't particularly planned. I didn't think it up. I knew I wanted to go into Human Resources from grad school. From there, I thought about a job I wanted to do. My focus was on doing good work. I had a performance mentality.

I've been fairly flexible and open. When I was told go do this, go do that, I did it. The only time I turned down a role was an opportunity to work in Asia. I was still single and I knew personally that I wanted to get married and have children. I felt that wouldn't happen if I went to Asia so I turned down the role. I said no because personally it wasn't right for me. I said yes to opportunities because I needed experiences. In the end, if you're not loving what you do, look to do something else.

Some advice I received early on in my career was, "If you're not nervous or anxious about a job, it's not a big enough stretch." To this day, that has turned out to be really good advice for me and TRUE. At Hyatt, there are 110K people and I am the Chief Human Resource Officer.

How Taking Risks Impacted Malaika's Career Journey
Taking risks has been critical, both in terms of taking on roles that were beyond my comfort zone, and in the work

itself. I remember when I recommended a transparent succession planning process at Diageo. Everyone thought I was crazy, but when we did it with no ripples, it felt amazing!

Avoiding Responsibility for One's Career
I definitely avoided conflict. I had some good coaching (woodshed moments) from several leaders who helped me see the harm I was doing by not being willing to state my view and deal with the consequences of it straight on.

The Formula for Owning Your Career
I think it is 10 parts hard work/performance plus a dose of flexibility, that is, being open to experiences you gain. In addition, find a coach or mentor who can help you plan along the way.

My advice for owning your career:
1. Decide what you want to do. Describe it around what you are particularly good at. What excites you? What motivates you? Say to yourself, "I'd like to solve these problems," and for whom. Write a description of that.
2. Socialize your vision with people you know and trust. If they are doing the job today, ask them how they got to where they are today.
3. In the meantime, continue to perform and deliver.
4. Create a picture for yourself. Create that vision. What does it look like? Make it real and tangible so it can compel you to take action.

5. Create leadership possibilities in your career. What is the biggest possibility you can achieve as a leader? Write it down. There is power in writing it down.

Key Relationships
To be successful, you need the following people on your team: mentors, an advocate or sponsor, and a great peer network to balance thoughts and share with.

Mentoring and Sponsorships as Career Levers
To me sponsorship and advocates are synonymous. They are the person in the room when you're not.

Sharing Career Successes
I try to tell my story as much as I can to people early in their careers—the good, the bad and the ugly—and I hope that they hear something that helps them along their journey.

Valuable Online Tools for Career Management
The online space can level the playing field. In terms of your career path, you can talk to people. Today, you can get a wider view by trolling LinkedIn. Ask people what jobs they did along the way. If you use the online space, you have a huge advantage. There is more transparency about roles that are out there now that we have those resources. Vast numbers of roles are filled by networking and referrals. I landed Hyatt through a headhunter. For senior-level roles, there's value in taking that call. Just grab coffee to establish relationship with someone. Headhunters are good advisors in terms of careers.

Career Advice

Be open to new experiences. Think about what you get out of them. Get sponsors/advocates to help you.

Nancy Di Dia
Chief Diversity and Inclusion Officer, Executive Director
Americas, Head, Diversity, Inclusion, Culture &
Engagement
Boehringer Ingelheim

I first met Nancy many years ago when she received an
award of excellence for her work in diversity at the Southern
Connecticut chapter of the Society for Human Resources
Management. I remember reaching out to connect with her
and found such a warm, authentic human being. We met and
had lunch and a friendship bloomed from the experience. I
would later get the opportunity to work with her and her
team.

The Story
I began my career in the banking industry as a teller at Dime
Savings Bank. I graduated from high school six months early
and attended community college. I then transferred to all-
female college in Troy, NY. I decided after three months that
it wasn't the place for me. As a result, I came back home, got
engaged to be married, and attended college part time. I
entered the workforce in the banking field at Chemical Bank
(which later became JP Morgan Chase). I ended up spending
the bulk of my career in the banking industry until I moved
into consulting, which landed me the opportunity to craft a
job description for the role I'm in today: modeling the way
as a thought leader and innovator in the diversity and
inclusion space.

Career Defining Moments

1. I worked my way up to the vice president level at age 29 and stayed with the bank until I was 40 years old.

2. I had some not-so-great managers (#metoo experiences) that caused me to want to champion those marginalized and underrepresented. I was asked to lead an LGBT group. I was the first openly gay woman who agreed to be part of an ERG. I championed the domestic partner coverage conversation, which led to an invitation to be on the National Diversity Council for the Bank. I represented views as a gay woman in my organization. I became co-chair of Pride Group.

3. I was then asked to consider a role as Head of Diversity, Tri-State & Texas. I agreed and moved from the business into HR.

4. Amidst sports injuries and a cancer diagnosis, and continual business changes, I left the bank in 2004 to start my own consulting firm, Di Dia Diversity Consulting Group, LLC.

5. I was hired by Boehringer Ingelheim as a consultant to help build their Diversity and Inclusion Strategy and ERG Strategy in 2006 after two years as a senior consultant with the Futurework Institute.

6. I was hired as a director in 2006 and was promoted to Chief Diversity Officer in 2009. The rest is history.

Owning Your Career

I have always taken on roles that inspired me (i.e. business development, sales, marketing). I was always curious to learn more. I created my own personal advisory board to ask opinions on career decisions. This enabled me to get a variety of opinions. I always considered the different perspectives given, processed the information, and then decided which way I would go.

How Taking Risks Impacted Nancy's Career Journey

I always put myself out there in risky situations when I had no experience, but I thought it was cool and ground breaking. I wanted to be on the leading edge of technology, following the trends. The older I got, the riskier I became in search of gaining experiences. I was more willing to try different things. I had less impostor syndrome going on.

The Formula for Owning Your Career

Believe in your capabilities; know your strengths and blind spots. Be self-aware and humble. Ask for help when you need it.

Key Relationships

I have been most responsible for my career. I'm my own advocate. In the workplace, sponsors supported or recommended me. My family was very encouraging (My life partner/wife, my sister, and my deceased parents). My home life enabled me to do what I needed to do to be successful. There was positivity, not resentment, in support of my own growth and development. I also had friends who were very encouraging.

Mentoring and Sponsorship as Career Levers

It's a personal decision. We all need advocates. Sometimes with sponsors, they move around or leave. It's important to have more than one sponsor. Socialize your talent. Let other leaders know who you are. It's important you are known to many, not a few.

Sharing Career Successes

I don't share my career successes unless I'm asked. Given my role, I get opportunities to share my journey. I write articles that allow me to share my expertise. I believe in the team concept. I will take full accountability if things go wrong but when they go right, I share the glory. I share successes in context of team wins and impact on business. I empower people on my team to be the best they can be.

Valuable Online Tools for Career Management

LinkedIn, Twitter, and Facebook. I am the company spokesperson on Diversity and Inclusion.

Career Advice

- Be patiently persistent.
- Reach out to as many people as you can to help you.
- Recognize your capabilities and own it.
- When in doubt, do the Amy Cuddy power pose. Know your power and use it in ways to make a difference.
- Be your best fan.

Joseph Santana
Executive, Coach, and Senior Leadership Advisor
Joseph Santana LLC

I had the pleasure of meeting Joe at a Diversity Best Practices Network Affinity Leadership Congress in 2014. He was facilitating a session on How to Leverage Employee Resource Groups to Drive Inclusion in an Organization. I remember thinking, wow, this guy is pretty sharp. He's someone I've followed over the years. We don't speak often, but I knew without a shadow of a doubt that his story was one I wanted to include in *The Power of Owning Your Career.* You will certainly be enthralled by his story and the sage advice that he imparts.

The Story
I'm from Brooklyn, New York, and if anybody told me I'd be doing what I'm doing today years ago, I would've probably gotten a good laugh and thought that they had a vivid imagination.

I started out originally on the business side. I actually took accounting in school and found that to be somewhat of an interesting topic to learn about but not an interesting thing to do on a day-to-day basis. I started switching over, and I got more involved in the business side.

I was originally the leader of a group of people in the outsourcing space. I led an outsourcing operation for Siemens. I had about 300 employees in that operation. One of the things that I found while I was in that work was how difficult it was in some cases to be able to fill open job seats, especially as the demographics were changing in the environment around me. I really got interested in learning more about what was going on, how would you get better people, and all that stuff. The net of it is that I ended up discovering how in many cases, we got in our own way due to our own unconscious biases, due to just the habit of doing things a certain way. That resulted in my driving a team of managers who reported in to me toward making changes to that. It made us more effective in bringing in the kind of people that we needed to succeed in meeting our business goals.

In doing that work, I discovered a passion for it and that it was really something that I found interesting. It was a way of opening the door and creating more opportunity for more people, and at the same time, I was meeting a business need. So later on, when the company was looking for someone to be their first D&I officer across the United States, I had no trouble at all accepting that nomination and that became my new role. I did that for a number of years and had a measure of success in that area due to having some great teams and leaders and people working with me. Then later on, I discovered that I love talking about this topic and teaching other people about it.

How Taking Risks Impacted Joseph's Career Journey

I always saw risk as being inherent to everything. Sometimes there might be a feeling that if we don't do something, or that if we play it safe that we are avoiding risk. But I think that risk is just part of living, so my own philosophy is that no matter what you do or don't do, you are taking some form of a risk, and since risk is not something that you can choose not to take, make your risk choice consciously. Make a choice in something, place your bet, because there is no such thing as not betting and keeping the money you've got in your pocket. You are betting one way or the other. So, pick a position and then pursue that position. In everything I did, I looked at what outcome I wanted. I thought, what is it that I think is the right thing that needs to be done here in order to produce the most value and the best situation for all those stakeholders? And then I would move forward, whether that was perceived by some people as being as riskier than not doing anything. I don't think I ever focused on that as much as getting from point A to point B.

The Formula for Owning Your Career

Wanting to make sure that, hey, am I enjoying this? Because when I enjoy things, I'm fully engaged. I'm more engaged than if I'm just going through moves without commitment or passion. That's why I am always asking myself: Am I creating value? Am I really creating true value that's measurable, that is perceived by people who are the recipients of whatever work product I put out there? And am I doing it in a fair way? Is it fair to myself and all the others involved?

Key Relationships

I think that a lot of the people who have helped shape my journey and to inform the approaches I use to manage and to work with people are from so many walks of life, both from my personal life as well as in business. My mom especially was a very strong, valued person, so one of the things I learned very early on in life is that you need to be true to yourself. You have to be authentic. You have to really believe in something, really give it your all in an honest and direct way.

I had lots of great managers who I worked for. Edmund, for example, was just so effective in the way that he conducted himself and in the way that he conducted business that I just basically said, "I'm going to study this guy, copy what he does, and then modify it a little bit as I go along to suit my own style." He was a mentor and a great role-model when it came to how to run a department and a group of people. He had this great mixture of integrity, know-how, with a certain amount of almost quiet humility that really worked well. And just his treatment of people in general was exemplary.

My wife, Eileen, is another person who I have to say contributes a lot. It's really funny, when I sit down with her and I say, "I've changed my mind. Instead of doing this, I'd rather go in this direction," she'll start asking questions like, "Are you sure about this?" and "What do you think about that?" And "Where does this take you? Is that where you want to go?" So, I've had the benefit of some solid in-home coaching as well in terms of my own development that way.

So, it's hard to put my finger on any one person, but there have been so many as I said both in my personal life as well as in my business life. And of course, there have been some examples of what not to do as well. I've worked for people where I know what they were trying to accomplish. And yet, I saw that everything they were doing was pushing people the other way. I made a mental note so when trying to generate similar results not to do that because that simply did not work. And what's more when it involves being outright mean to other people, it doesn't feel good to do that. In the end, I would say a combination of people in my personal life as well as in my business life, have shown me great qualities that made me say, "You know what? I want to be like that. I want to work towards that." Having that, recognizing these key people and then taking action to continue to develop a better version of myself certainly played a big part in leveraging those key relationships.

Most people, if they look around them, probably have a lot of candidates for a success team of teachers and role-models of their own. They might be relatives, spouses, friends, people they work with, subordinates, peers as well as managers or managers one level up from their immediate manager. I think that those people are there, you just have to look for them. And ultimately, I think that very early in someone's career, it's good to ask, "Who do I want to be and how I do want to show up in life? What are some of the things that are really important to me?" The answer to those questions will help you leverage those key relationships in the best possible way.

I think that you build everything around the focusing questions of, "What do I do for a living? Who do I do it for? Who do I look to learn from? And, I think all of that is informed by your own internal journey and how you want to show up in this life. Who is it that you want to be? Who do you want to serve? In my own career, when I was working inside organizations with a leader who was not someone who would basically support my career goals as I was supporting theirs, I made department changes and moved to other areas as nicely and diplomatically as I could. But I would try to basically pick my bosses or my leaders, to make sure that they were people that I could work with effectively who would also be good for my career, just as I would be good for theirs.

Sharing Career Successes

Sharing your career successes will always pay off. I've actually had speaking engagements and other work come to me as a result of somebody that I mentored or coached, or who read one of my articles or attended a program I conducted bringing me up to someone else who was looking for some particular service that I provide. So, in a way that giving and sharing creates ambassadors who help to share who you are and what you do.

Valuable Online Tools for Career Management

I use LinkedIn, Twitter, Facebook and other platforms. Prior to these platforms being as ubiquitous as they are now, years ago, I also did a fair amount of writing. So, one of the things that I did that I think was really of value career-wise for me was that I became a sharer. So, if I was successful in putting together a practice or a procedure that really worked well, whether it was in the IT space or in the Diversity and Inclusion space, I would contribute written articles and white papers in how-to formats for magazines and ezines that would help other people copy my approaches. When I was working with large organizations, this also got me internal recognition since my writing also positioned them as thought-leaders in these particular areas.

Career Advice

I think it's important to really personally engage in the things you do. You should feel a connection and passion for the value that you're creating and enjoy the creative process. You should also be focused on how to bring value to all these other people that are part of your team. The more you do for others, the more they do for you.

But I think it has to come from a very sincere place of really caring about their success and ensuring that you become part of their success formula. Of these people that you're working with and helping rise through the ranks, I would say 99.9% are going to bring you along with them because you're part of their success team.

I think young professionals also need to know when it's time to fire their boss. If you are in a relationship with a boss that is one-sided, or where you're not getting any value out of the effort, or you're not moving in the direction that you have laid out for yourself, you need to look for somebody else. It might be that person's nature is such that they're not the giving type, or they're not the type who will support those who support them. That's fine. That's their journey, but you need to move on at that point and look for a more productive relationship. Perhaps you'll find it in another department, or another organization. Or maybe, if you decide to strike it out on your own as I did years ago, in a partner. On a final personal note, I highly recommend making "striking it out on your own" one of your ultimate goals. For me, its been the most rewarding step of all.

Havilah Malone
Author, Entrepreneur, Former Ms. Louisiana

I met Havilah earlier this year in a Mastermind Group that I joined with the National Speakers Association. Because of that, I began following her on social media and began to learn more about her mantra of being proof of what's possible. Her empowerment messages resonated with me causing me to see a fit as one of the interview profiles I planned to share in *The Power of Owning Your Career*. Her story is fun, informative, and awe-inspiring. I know you will enjoy reading her profile.

The Story
I graduated from high school at 16, I graduated from college at 19, and when I went to college my degrees were in Dramatic Arts and Communications. I minored in Psychology.

From a young age, I knew I loved being on the acting stages, or being on television-type stages, but I did not know all the turns and twists that my career would take me on. I also equally loved the mindset piece, and just understanding why people did what they did. I think from a young age, we come here kind of knowing what it is that we love or what it is that we want, we just don't know how it's going to show up in the world.

So, after leaving college, I actually went into television. I worked in production and in the news for a couple of years.

Then I found that, you know what, this isn't really my thing. Every day a rape, a murder, or fire, followed by another report of a rape, a murder, or fire — I thought, this isn't quite it, but I still like this television platform.

Through a series of different opportunities that had opened up to me, I ended up going into Corporate America. I hadn't previously seen that in my map of reality, going down that lane, but I think one of the biggest things is being open to the opportunities that present themselves, being open to new doors. I'm so grateful for that experience, and the skill sets that I learned; like being in management, working with varying clients around the country, and working with teams of people. The things I was able to learn have served me in every aspect of my life and in different career moves that I have made.

From there, while I was working for Hewlett-Packard, they found out about my television background and so I was offered the opportunity to represent them on HSN, QVC, Shop at Home TV, and America Store. The piece of me that desires that television aspect was able to be fulfilled in some way. Life will make a way when you allow your skill or your gift or what you're passionate about to be known and you put it out there.

Today I am a number one best-selling author of a book called *How to Become a Publicity Magnet in Any Market Via TV, Radio, and Print.* I was able to take my television background as well as my business background, and share with people how they can take a message, service, or product and put it out there on a very large stage so that they can make a bigger impact and how to do it for free.

Career Defining Moments

When Hewlett-Packard went through their huge layoff, which was in 2012, they were deciding whether they were going to break off the printing and computing side of their business. Our entire organization ended up being laid off. It could've been devastating and very hard, and for most people a layoff is viewed that way. It actually ended up being a blessing in disguise, because sometimes I feel like we go down a path and that path has had its season. You will learn the lessons you need to learn; you have the experience you need to have, and it's now time to move into the next season of your life or your career. For me, God had to push me out of the nest because I wasn't going to leave.

That was a huge defining moment for me, because even though I was very comfortable in my job and made great money with a great company and wonderful people who I worked with, I wasn't happy. I would literally wake up every day depressed. So, it was time. I had learned the things that I needed to learn, I had the experiences I needed to have, and now it was time to take that skill set and move on to my next phase of life. The layoff gave me an opportunity, because I had kind of lost myself in that whole shuffle. My identity had become tied up with being with HP. I had gotten away from what Havilah loves; what Havilah is passionate about. This gave me an opportunity to do some soul searching and personal development work.

I literally took about two years and started working on me. I started working with Tony Robbins, I actually joined his Platinum Partnership Program. We traveled around the world with Tony, learning from him, and attending all of his public training events and some exclusive private events too.

That opened me up to delving more into the psychology side, that psychology piece that I also am very passionate about. Understanding how we work and how we are able to utilize our power to create anything we want. That also led me to breaking my silence around being abused when I was younger, being sexually molested, and healing from that. That pain became a platform for the next phase of my career, because I went into empowerment speaking and helping people to truly own their power and own their lives. Everything that happens along our path is literally helping us to unfold who we are, who we're supposed to be, and how we're supposed to show up. That has been very evident through the shifts and the roads that I have taken in my career.

How Taking Risks Impacted Havilah's Career Journey
For a kid, riding a bike could seem like the biggest task in the world. And even though it's exciting and it looks like it's fun, when you first get on the bike and try to ride it, you keep falling off. So, for you to keep getting back on the bike is taking a risk. But once you finish scraping your knee, once you wobble around a little bit, you fall a few more times, you start to learn and get the hang of it, and you get the skill of it. And you start moving along, then you get the enjoyment of, "Ah! I accomplished this. I did it, wow! It's actually fun doing this and I'm good at it now." This applies to everything

in life. Because everything is new until you do it. I think taking risks is about becoming comfortable with being uncomfortable. And when you can get to that place, you realize everything you want is on the other side of your comfort zone, then you're going to be good.

Avoiding Responsibility for One's Career

I always wanted to be on camera. When I started working for FOX, I started as a production assistant then moved up as a field producer and continued to move up behind the scenes. And I never took the initiative to go on camera because I thought I wasn't pretty enough. I thought I didn't have the skill sets that were needed. I didn't think I was the right image to be on television even though that was actually my passion: to be on camera sharing the information. So, for a very long time in my television career I just played small.

Now I'm going to put a caveat in there. The skill sets that I learned behind the scenes were priceless and I'm so grateful for them. Everything on your path does work out for your good. But sometimes we just delay where we're supposed to be.

Now, moving forward, I was an assistant casting director on this one project with AMC. We were casting for commentators for *A Long, Hot Summer* with Paul Newman and Joanne Woodward. We were casting commentators who were going to talk about different scenes in the movie. They kind of pop up during the movie as it's being aired.

The main casting director and I had all of these people coming in for the audition. I kept watching these people, thinking, that's where I'm supposed to be. I have been holding back, but that's what I'm passionate about doing.

To tie in the whole mentor piece, we took lunch and the main casting director came up to me, and she said, "Havilah, I really think you should audition for this." At first I was super excited and I'm like, oh my God, this could be my opportunity, here's my chance. And then that voice came back up in my mind, that voice of self-doubt, that voice of sabotage came up. It was like, "Nope, you're not good enough." At the time I weighed more, so I told myself, "You're overweight. They're not going to want to see you on TV. You have got all these talented people coming to audition. You're not good enough."

So, I told the casting director, "No, no thank you. I don't think this is good for me, plus we have all these people auditioning." I denied the opportunity. We went back after lunch, and as the next group of people came in to audition, that passion flared up in me again. I'm like, "I should be doing this. What are you doing, Havilah?"

We get all the way down to the end of the day and the casting director comes up to me one more time. "Havilah, I really think you should audition for this." And I literally in that moment had this internal battle. I had this fight with myself where one side was saying, "Just do it," and the other side was saying, "No, you're not going to get it, so why even try?" But, I finally agreed. I said, "You know what, all right, cool,

I'll do it." So, I stood on the same line that everybody else had been standing on. I answered the questions that they were asking, and then we wrapped up for the day. After two weeks had passed I was just like, "You're so stupid. Why did you even do that? You're not going to get it. That was just a waste of time."

I was being down on myself and I got a phone call. That phone call was from the main casting director and she said, "I have some news for you." And I'm thinking she's about to tell me we that we need to do another round of auditions to bring some more people in because they didn't find what they were looking for. And instead she tells me I had been chosen as one of the commentators on the project, in fact I was chosen as the lead commentator. And I was like, "Oh my God!"

The Formula for Owning Your Career

I think that taking ownership of your career is really about deciding what it is that you're passionate about, what it is that you love and brings you joy, or fills your cup, and then being open to and even pursuing ways to make that a reality. I do believe that the things that you love to do, the things that you would literally do for free, are the very things that you should be getting paid the most for. A lot of times, what I find is that because we love to do it, we don't require the payment for it. People accept less or settle for less because they tell themselves, "Oh, because that comes easy to me," or because, "I love doing it so much, I should just give it away for free." No, that's the very thing that you should be soaring to the top of your industry with, making the top dollars doing, because that's where your skills lie and it's your gift that you're giving to the world.

I think the formula would be first, listening to that internal voice. It's listening to our own internal voice and not all the external voices that try to guide us in the direction that they want our life to go. Each of us has been given a gift, and that gift is our life. And our life paths could be very, very different from the well-meaning people who we could be surrounded with who are always offering advice. We weren't meant to fit into a mold or a box, we should own that first and foremost. That you are unique, you are different and your path may not look like everybody else's.

So, I think first listening to your own internal guidance and then making a decision. Decide what you want and then take a step. Just start by taking one step. You don't have to know how it's all going to look. Quite frankly, you're not going to know how it's all going to look because that's not your job. That's God's job.

So, your *job* is to make the decision and then once you get the guidance or you get the hunch or the idea, take a step. And then continue to learn, continue to educate yourself, continue to ask people who are qualified to give you answers. People can give you advice for free all day long. Make sure the advice you're getting is from people who are qualified to give you that advice.

There's a book I love, which is George S. Clason's *The Richest Man in Babylon.* Through that Clason shares the example of Arkad, the character in the book. Arkad asks for advice on buying diamonds from ship people. People who have nothing to do with the diamond business. So, he gives the ship merchants his money, when they came back to his dismay, he learned that they had sold him fake stuff.

If you want to know about buying diamonds, go to a diamond dealer. If you want to know about building a technology company, go to somebody in that field. If you want to know about getting into management in a Fortune 500 company, then go to somebody who has been there, and done that; someone who is qualified and can give you advice worth taking.

I think the last thing would be to just be open minded. Be open that things may not show up exactly like the picture you have in your mind. We don't know enough about any given subject to be closed minded. We don't, because things could show up as unicorns. And you'll be like, "Wait, I didn't even know that existed. I didn't even know that was a possibility. I couldn't even have thought that up or imagine that happening that way." So just be open minded.

Key Relationships

I have been brought some really instrumental people throughout my career. When I was working with Hewlett Packard, I had a friend, colleague, and mentor. Lori Stewart was one of my colleagues who was so supportive and nurturing of not only my career but other aspects of my life as well. She introduced me to a healthy lifestyle. She was one of my angels during my HP time. Then when I was in Television, I had other people who were catalysts for me. They were those angels who helped give me a new perspective or give me a tool, or give me a mindset shift that helped to propel me forward. That has been long-lasting. I can literally think of somebody in every single thing that I've done that has helped me along the way.

Mentoring and Sponsorships as Career Levers

Sponsors are a necessity, they're a must. We need people who believe in us because we so often struggle with belief in ourselves. And struggle with our own self-worth and that self-love. When you have somebody who can mentor you, who can say, "Look, this is the road that I would suggest." Or, "This is the turn that you should make." Or, "You know what, you are good enough. Yes, I believe in you, go for it, I'm here to support you. You have questions, come and ask me. I've been down that road before." So, we need that and we need the people who will say, "You know what, I believe in this thing that you're creating and I'll put my money behind it. I'll send you to school, I'll pay for that class for you. I'll support your conference or your event and I'll sponsor a table. I'll sponsor a stage." Yes, we all need that. And we need to become that for somebody else.

My mom was my sponsor when I executive produced and hosted a talk show. That was my first time taking on a full project myself and not having a big network behind me or having somebody else doing it. So, I learned a lot of lessons because I didn't know what the heck I was doing. I was also bleeding out money because I didn't realize how expensive it was going to be to do it. So, my mom stepped up and she said, "I believe in you." So, she went out and bought me this new, top-of-the-line Mac Pro Notebook and Final Cut 10, which is a top of the line film editing system. She got me all the additional hard drives and components I needed. It was a $5,000 investment. We were able to finish the season of the show, when my original editor dropped the ball. Thank God for all of that behind-the-scenes training I got working in TV, including becoming a certified editor. Every experience and every lesson has its purpose.

Another one of my sponsors was Saundra Richardson. When I would be at my lowest of lows and I was trying to recreate myself and just rebuild myself and decide what I wanted to do, she was there. I thought, now I have all these skills, I have all these passions. What direction should I go into first? And Saundra would always be there to support and nurture my dreams and give me the pep talk I needed to keep going.

So, heck yes, you need people who believe in you, who will give you information and boost you up and confirm your greatness. And you need people who are going to put their dollars behind you.

Valuable Online Tools for Career Management
I would recommend Upwork.com for all of your freelance employee needs; from graphic designers, to editors, illustrators, transcriptionists, executive assistants, and so much more! Another valuable tool is social media. Whatever your platform of preference is, whether that's Instagram,

Facebook, LinkedIn, or Twitter, social media is such a huge part of advancing your career at this point in our technological age. That is because people will go online to find you, your conversations, and the image that you are portraying in this social sphere. They will also look at the things that you're doing or organizations that you are a part of. I've had so many doors open for me; from acting jobs to speaking jobs to relationships, because of social media. Because of having an online presence and being myself and sharing my skills, sharing my life with people on social media. That is such a powerful tool in our day and age that must be utilized.

Career Advice

Figure out who you are and what you want. What makes you happy? What do you feel like you want your legacy to be? What do you want your impact on this world to be? And go and do that. Just be open. Be open to the doors and opportunities that present themselves and say yes. Even if it's scary, even if you feel like you're not ready. If you feel like, "You know what. I need to go and take another class." Or, "I need to go ask 15 people whether I should do it." No. Trust you. Trust your internal guidance system and say, "Yes!"

Marc Stephenson Strachan
Chairman, ADCOLOR, Inc.
Former EVP, Chief Client Officer, Publicis.Sapient, &
Former VP Corporate Relations and Constituent Affairs,
Diageo North America

Marc Strachan is the man. I do not say that lightly. What a joy it was to meet him during my time at Diageo. When he amazes me, I tell him he's the man. That's because he has an amazing track record and when you look at his body of work, you can see that he's done some incredible things. As Chair of the African Heritage Employees (AHEAD) Employee Resource Group, I worked with Marc to bring the Alvin Ailey dance troupe to Diageo in celebration of Black History Month. What a joy it is to reflect back on bringing such rich culture into an organization. His legacy remains intact with standout career moves like spearheading the marketing partnership between Sean Combs and Diageo to up level the Ciroc Brand. Not only is he an innovator, but he masterfully owns his career. I know you will enjoy his story.

The Story
A) My story is pretty much like most. I am the son of hard-working, yet very loving parents. I had great support as a young man, and I was given a lot of encouragement and pushed to chase my dreams and build a career opportunity.

B) A key highlight was that I was always able to build bridges with people and connect with them in positive ways: teachers, professors, fellow students, teammates, etc. This afforded me access to people who would help me at various points on my personal and career journey. A major early highlight was my receiving a fellowship from the American Association of Advertising Agencies (the 4A's). This was my entry into the world of advertising and marketing. This changed the trajectory of my career and life.

C) After my fellowship, I was hired by an African American VP of production at a major advertising agency to work as a production assistant. He liked my interview. From there I worked hard, learned many key aspects of the production and creative sides of the business, and was eventually accepted into the training program for account management. I ultimately became an account director.

D) After a couple of years of moving up, I left the agency business for the first time to take a role in marketing at The Block Drug Company. I knew I needed better marketing skills. It was a huge change, and a huge learning curve for me. I struggled in the beginning, but again, my ability to build relationships helped me find people who agreed to assist me. I learned fast, got promoted, and by chance, met a man at an industry dinner. He offered me a position at his company that would bring me back into advertising. I was made a vice president at the Mingo Group, an African American owned and operated agency. This gave me introductions to a diverse group of business leaders on many fronts and opened the door to my career in the world of spirts and beer, as I was assigned to manage the Miller Brewing Company and the Joseph E. Seagram's Company accounts. This is critical, for it once again provided me with opportunities to build special relationships. I was able to build on those relationships later, for example when I worked on the Schieffelin & Somerset business before it became a part of Diageo. My connections and contacts there were the same people who opened the door for me to be hired at Diageo, where I had a great career run. **RELATIONSHIPS ARE KEY!**

Owning Your Career

- I learned to embrace my passions. I try to do things that I am passionate about.
- I am honest with myself, and authentic with others.
- I am clear in my desires, intentions, and goals to the people whom I work with and report to, and have an impact, direct or indirect, on my career. I call it "helping the helpers helps me."
- I set development plans for my career and identifying the areas that I have needed to improve in annually. Everyone needs to improve, consistently and sustainably. YOU GROW THROUGH LEARNING!

How Taking Risks Impacted Marc's Career Journey

Taking risks is not something that everyone is comfortable with or trained to embrace. As a matter of fact, most people are trained to be risk averse. Taking educated risks proved to be game changing for me. It allowed me to reap significant performance gains when I was successful, and to learn valuable lessons when I wasn't. However, taking risks is also a product of one's environment. Some companies and employers reward risk takers. However, the majority do not. **NO PAIN, NO GAIN!**

Avoiding Responsibility for One's Career

I have always been one to take and accept responsibility for my actions. There was a time when I was in a position where I refused to take responsibility. My direct manager had given me verbal approval to proceed with authorizing a significant spend against a client's budget. I moved forward with the spend. I sent out all the relevant authorizations under my name and executed the transaction. A week later, the client called me directly, and gave me a serious tongue lashing. He advised that he had spoken to my manager, who advised him that I had moved forward with the spend authorization without his knowledge or approval. The client advised that he did not want to execute that expenditure, and stated that as he did not authorize the agency to move forward, the agency (in this case ME), would be responsible for the expense. It was a significant amount of money, and I was facing being fired. It was my word against my manager's. However, due to my past track record of diligence, performance, and rigor, the head of the division decided to give me a break. The agency and client agreed to split the cost of the expense, and I was "penalized" by losing about six months of eligibility towards a promotion.

I learned a valuable lesson from that episode: 1) not everyone is honest and will do the right thing when their own self-preservation may be in jeopardy. 2) Never move forward without some sort of written confirmation, even if you must send a confirming note to someone. I was so adamant about this for the rest of my career, that I would make people sign a cocktail napkin if I had to. Some people didn't like it when I insisted they comply, but they all understood. I was not playing! Protect yourself first and foremost!

The Formula for Owning Your Career

Experience + self-awareness, with a pinch of self-assuredness, and a dash of authenticity and truth. Stir it up, put in a baking dish, and nurture. Know and be true to yourself!

Key Relationships

There are several people who have been responsible for my success. Family members and professional colleagues are among them. And myself. People can only open the doors and provide you with the runway. You must drive your success by performing well and delivering against your goals. My college marketing professor, my first boss, the first African American man I worked for, and two of my clients that have become great personal friends have contributed to my success. All of them have had a fingerprint on my career. I also always found out what was important to the people on the other side of my relationships. Relationships are two-sided. Remember that.

Mentoring and Sponsorships as Career Levers

A mentor or a sponsor can be the difference between getting noticed, moving ahead, and being invited to sit at the right tables. However, not everyone needs one or has one. Sometimes you might have general supporters, people who help facilitate your progress. Mentors generally work more like counsel, and as such, are not as impactful in getting you promoted. A sponsor generally "adopts" you and takes responsibility for you and your progress. A sponsor can and will speak on your behalf in certain situations. Know the difference and treat each with the respect they deserve!

Sharing Career Successes

I believe it is the responsibility of those of us who have had a modicum of (relative) success, to reach back and bring others forward. I share my career success by creating possibilities for others, mentoring and coaching those coming behind me, and by setting a good example of what a true leader is by being a good leader. Lead by example and support others along the way!

Valuable Online Tools for Career Management

Social media has proven to be a great tool. The simple reason is its reach, and the fact that you can tell your story to the people who matter to you most. You don't have to wait for a company press release (if they even put one out these days) on your career success, advancements, promotions, and achievements. You can put forth your own story: your new roles, changes of positions, new companies and such instantly and effectively. You can also share your POVs and opinions on industry-related matters in a personal setting that heretofore did not exist. People now can get to know you and what you believe in and stand for. You can also stay close to industry stakeholders and opinion leaders, and have your finger on the pulse with an extended community of decision makers, when opportunities arise (friends, colleagues, recruiters). Social media is a great tool. Use it wisely, for it can hurt you if misused!

Career Advice

My advice to anyone seeking to successfully own their career, is to do just that...own it! Unless you are extremely privileged, you had better understand that you are the main driver of your brand, your knowledge, your personality, your vision, and your career. Yes, others can directionally impact its course or trajectory, but at the very core, the very bottom line, the primary direction rests with you. Do you have a vision? Do you have a plan? Do you have the drive? Do you have the wherewithal to put in the work it takes, especially when things get tough and the road ahead looks dark and bleak? It is, in the final analysis, up to you. Now some luck and some good karma never hurt anyone. But you can't rely on those elements of the universe solely to get you to the finish line. You own your career. And you must protect, maintain, nurture, and drive it forward!

John Lahey
Former President
Quinnipiac University

I am a Quinnipiac Alumnus. During my freshman year at Quinnipiac, President Lahey was hired. My work study boss at the time was a part of the process for selecting the new president for the college. I always felt privileged to be present for what would turn into his 30-year plus legacy. Over the years, I ran into President Lahey at various events and up close as a member of the Quinnipiac Alumni Board of Governors. I was very curious about his story and was more than delighted that he agreed to let me interview him. I think you'll equally be delighted to learn from this icon about his career journey. He was gracious, humble, and an inspirational leader.

The Story

I grew up in an Irish household in New York City. And my father was a brick layer. He never went to college. My mom, believe it or not, was a college graduate back in the '20s when there were very few women going to school. She didn't work; she raised the family and I was the baby in the family growing up. Eventually she did go to work as an elementary school teacher.

I lived in a typical neighborhood for back then. The school and the church we went to were a couple blocks away so you went there and everyone knew you. And as I often joke, I thought everyone was Irish growing up because the teachers were all Irish, the priests were all Irish, the coaches, the Catholic youth, and they were all Irish.

It was a great place to grow up and you just felt the love and support. I lived in a house that my grandmother had bought. She moved in downstairs in the basement room and she had her two daughters on the next two floors, one of her daughters being my mom. I grew up in a house where my cousins were up on the second floor. My grandmother and grandfather were in the same house too with my mom and dad. There were three children in our family and my aunt had three children as well. So, as I said, we all went to the same schools, so the teachers all knew us, and we played in the same athletic league.

What I learned back then was, you work hard and you play hard. I always admired my dad. Brick laying was not easy work, and he worked very hard. But then on the weekends, he and my mom enjoyed sports and partying. So, you learned a lot about how to interact with other people. And you learned the full range of experience that people have.

It might have been parochial in the sense that, you know, we're all Catholic and we're all Irish and the lesson was we had a very emotionally supportive kind of environment. So, if you had a problem, you couldn't hide with it. Deal with it or whatever. So that was the environment I grew up in.

One thing I learned from my dad was hard work and what I learned from my mom was the importance of education. My mom pushed education. She wanted all of her kids to go to college and get a good education. So that started me off, and

I went from Catholic high school to Fordham Prep, which is a very good school in the Bronx, and then I went to the University of Dayton.

Starting out at college I was an English major. I think I probably selected it because of my mom. I admired and loved her. I had my first philosophy course when I was in sophomore year and that was the beginning of everything. I just took to philosophy like a fish to water. What I liked about philosophy was that I was always interested in conceptual things as opposed to more mundane sorts of practical things. That's probably still true to this day. But I like to define a philosopher as a conceptual cartographer. So, the logical relationships, sort of like a map maker, but in the world of ideas and concepts and so on.

And that's what I enjoyed about philosophy. And even back then, I wanted to know the big things, like "Why are we here? What's the purpose of being a human?" Or, "Where'd this Earth come from?" Or, "Where are we going when we leave this Earth?" I didn't think of them so much as philosophical until I really started studying philosophy. I just thought of it as probably religious or allegoric questions, but they were things that interested me.

Once I discovered philosophy, that was the end of it. I had one professor who reinforced in me that I could study philosophy and make a contribution. I was asking so many questions in class that he finally grabbed me after class, and he said, "Look, John, you know all this stuff we're doing here. I'll give you an A for the course, but you just come to my office once a week and spend two or three hours, and I'll give you some readings and we'll discuss those readings." It had such an impact on a 19-year-old kid. I didn't have any role models who were priests or lawyers or doctors or any college-educated people. So, this was a new experience for me. He was a professor who was very well thought of, he was a free thinker who was marrying evolution with philosophical thought which was radical at the time, at least for Catholics because they had a more static view things.

I switched my major to philosophy and I should have been more practical then and thought, "Well, what job am I going to get?" I don't remember my mom really challenging me or anything along those lines. She knew I was enjoying a major. Back then you could still get a college degree and eventually get a job, whereas today, you know, employers want someone with practical skills.

I concluded at some point, the only thing you could do with philosophy directly is to teach. So, it became clear to me at that point that I would have to think about not only getting a Bachelor's degree, but a Master's degree and a PhD. My goal became to be a college professor and I ultimately did that.

By the time I was in my senior year I applied to a couple places and actually stayed in Dayton for my Master's degree in Philosophy. I stayed there for six years. And then I was a graduate assistant so I taught for two years before I was accepted to the University of Miami for my PhD. I went there and completed my PhD in three years. In 1973, here I was, a 26-year-old kid with a PhD. I can still remember they handed me my diploma and the registrar said, "You look awfully young to be a Doctor of Philosophy."

Back then I was naive enough to think, well it's going to be Plato, Aristotle, and Lahey when they write the history of philosophy. But it didn't quite work out that way. In fact, it's funny, I just heard the expression in the past year or two when it was a pretty tough job market and someone said, "This was the worst job market for college professors since 1973." Which was the year that I graduated, of course, not realizing the job market was bad because colleges and universities had hired a lot of professors to educate my generation.

So, there were a lot of freshly minted PhDs at that time. The college professors were all hired and then the demographics plateaued in the nine-year period from '64 basically to '73. There wasn't a need, so much, for philosophers, believe it or not.

I had met my wife in Dayton. We got married and went to Miami before going back to New York. And I literally couldn't get a job. Instead, I spent that first year after I got a PhD in a warehouse in the Bronx working as a Teamster. And no one knew I had a PhD. I didn't put it on my application. The company I was working for was a big supermarket chain in New York. I had worked there in the summers doing the same kind of work I did when I was an undergraduate. I had also been working in a meat warehouse in the evenings when I was in my last year, finishing up my dissertation. And the day I defended my dissertation and they all congratulated me, "Dr. Lahey," I went to work that evening at this meat warehouse, slugging large chucks of meat, loading trucks and so on. And no one knew anything until I left. During that year there was one guy who worked there who sensed that I maybe had a little bit more intelligence than the average Teamster. "You know, Lahey," he said, "You're wasting your time. You can pass that sanitation test." I went home and told my wife that evening. I found it interesting that he only pegged me for being a garbage man. I was fortunate enough to finally get a job teaching in Alabama. George Wallace was governor at the time. This was 1974. I went down there and it was a different world for a kid coming from the Bronx.

It was a small college in Alabama about an hour north of Birmingham and my specialty was moral philosophy and social political philosophy. I figured I wouldn't stay very long in Alabama and that my next teaching job would hopefully be back in the Northeast. It became clear to me after my first year in Alabama that I might be there longer than I would like if I were just going to limit myself to teaching. So, it was at that point that I got exposure to the broader career opportunities in higher education. I decided to go and get another degree.

I had a Bachelor's, a Master's and a PhD, all in philosophy. I decided to get a Master's degree in higher education administration at Columbia. I applied to Columbia and I got in their program. I completed an MA in higher education administration in 1977.

My thinking was that there were a lot more jobs in higher education in administration. Many, many more, versus teaching philosophy. And so, I thought, "Well, maybe my best hope of getting out of Alabama is to get an administrator job, where I could still continue to teach a class." Most administrators taught if they had a PhD. So, I could still spend my life on a college campus, which is what I liked to do, and I could still teach philosophy, although obviously not on a full-time basis. And so, that was kind of my thinking at the time.

Career Defining Moments

In my third year in Alabama, I was teaching an ethics course: abortion, capital punishment, racism, privacy...a lot of hot-button ethical and moral topics of the time. I thought it would be interesting, and college students back then were interested in some of those things. I found students were less interested in philosophy and high-level conceptual cartography the way I was. It didn't dissuade me from the importance of philosophy, but it's always better if you're teaching something to students who are really interested, and not just because it's a course they have to take, or some requirement to fulfill. Philosophy has a pretty small market of people who are really interested in that, or at least that's been my experience.

I contacted the Warden at Draper Prison, which is in Montgomery, Alabama. I told him what my idea was, and he agreed to let me teach. I taught a course in Draper Prison one night a week for 12 weeks. I wanted to teach a course for people for whom capital punishment and racism and abortion are not theoretical.

I drove two and a half hours there and drove two and a half hours back on little country roads. When you walked into that prison, there were four wings. You walk in, and there's a wing with 250 inmates in bunk beds next to one another. On the other side as you walk, there were 250 inmates on this side. You go down a little bit, another 250, and another 250. A thousand inmates packed into it like sardines if you can imagine.

When you drive down to Montgomery, as far as the eye could see, it's snow white. I had never seen cotton before. These were cotton fields that were just in bloom, in full, and it was just white all over. 90% of the inmates were African American. 100% of the guards were white. This was a serious prison. They had guys toting guns, and rifles, and so on. What job did they have these inmates doing? Picking cotton.

The job that opened up in the third year that got me back to New York was the director of the Marist College Green Haven program. The Green Haven Correctional Facility is outside of Poughkeepsie. I have no doubt, had I not taught that course in Draper Prison that year, I wouldn't have gotten this job as director of the Marist Green Haven program. That was my first full-time administrative job. Then I became associate dean for continuing education. Then I became executive assistant to the president. Then the next year, I became vice president for development. I was in that for five years. Then they made me executive vice president, chief operating officer. They wanted me to stay to be the next president, thinking at the time that the president would retire soon, but he was fairly young himself. I stayed in that position for two years, and that's when the Quinnipiac position came along.

How Taking Risks Impacted John's Career Journey

I'm sure I've taken risks but I think I've taken what I would consider at least calculated risks that had a reasonably good chance for success. And yet, I certainly went into it with my eyes open.

Aristotle defines courage. He says, "Courage is midway between cowardice and foolhardiness." Probably some of those might have been on the foolhardy side. I don't know, I guess you're right, I was certainly open to new experiences. Even when I went to the University of Dayton, that was kind of unheard of. Most of my fellow graduates from Fordham Prep either went to Fordham, Holy Cross, or Boston College. Almost none of them went west of the Hudson. And I didn't know anyone. My mom put me on the train with a little suitcase or whatever. I had just barely turned 18.

I'm optimistic and open to new experiences. I think of things that I would like to see happen, and I'm optimistic that I'm going to succeed in having those things happen. I'm sure I've had some failures here and there, but none that I can really think of that I took personally at least. There were times there that some people, including my wife, were trying to get me at least to think, "Maybe I ought to do something different." I could have had a job at McGraw Hill, but the idea of selling books didn't appeal to me as a 26-year-old. That wasn't why I got a PhD. I wanted to write the books, not sell the books.

I did become a little more practical. After you have a child, after you get married, you get a little more practical. But then just getting that first administrative job, really, from there it just took care of itself. Unbeknownst to me at the time, I was pretty good at administration. I was pretty good at management. I was pretty good at business.

Key Relationships

Well, having a happy partner helps. Judy and I fell in love in my junior year in college when she was in her third year in nursing school. It was her final year. But we met on a blind date and just fell in love and we've been married 48 years. It's amazing how many really successful business people are married to the same person. I do think having a partner who supports you and again, you enjoy experiencing life with, is very important. And certainly, to be a college president, that's very much a partnership. Judy goes to as many events as I do, and evenings and weekends, I'll be with parents going to a concert tonight or out there for parents' weekends. To be a successful university president, you certainly need a partner.

It's pretty healthy to keep a level head to go home to a wife who tells you to take the garbage out. Or then when you have kids, they couldn't care less. I'm not President Lahey, I'm just Dad. And they value your time.

Mentoring and Sponsorships as Career Levers

I'd like to tell you I had a lot of mentors. I had people who were helpful to me in a lot of ways. I won't say that any one person was helpful, but a lot of people were helpful because I always got along with people.

I always went looking for people who were older than me or ahead of me. Even when I made the basketball team in elementary school, I was the only one in the sixth grade who made it on to the eighth-grade team. And I was so proud of that. But the gap between a 12-year-old and a 14-year-old is huge. I learned a lot like that. In all the jobs I've had, I looked at people who were older than I was. What were they doing?

As I said, my philosophy professor had a lot to do with my going into philosophy in the first place and falling in love with it. And learning what other people do. So, I just had a general sense that this was a better way to go.

Career Advice

I actually think my success has more to do with the philosopher in me. From the very beginning, get a clear concept about where you want to go and what you want to accomplish. Communicate that to all the people you know in order to help you achieve that, and get out of their way. All those lessons I learned from philosophy, whether it was the Oracle of Delphi or Plato's view of justice.

I think having a little bit of humility is a good thing. In particular, realizing that while you might know a lot about something, there are a lot of areas out there you know nothing about. Being willing to take advice and direction when it's outside of your area is extremely important.

Tomiko Fraser-Hines
Model/Actress

I've known about Tomiko since a while back. I remembered her work from the pages of magazines as a girl who looked like me in the Maybelline advertisements. She was an inspiration. What particularly appealed to me were the similarities we shared in our messaging for women's empowerment. She inspires and fully embraces her authentic self and is not afraid to share it. In the past year, I reconnected with her via social media. It was nice to see her still progressing and being so open with her story of infertility challenges, and re-entering the modeling space later in life. Her story is filled with inspiration and you will feel her warmth exude from her profile filled with wisdom. I know you will enjoy reading it.

The Story
I always had aspirations of modeling from a young age and they weren't really my own personal aspirations, they were more people saying, "She's so tall! She's so thin!" From the age of eleven I've been over 5'8". I was almost 5'9" when I was twelve years old so I've always been tall and thin. It was never anything that I gave serious thought to. I've always wanted to be a teacher. I remember being in grade school and just loving learning. I loved reading and was really fond of school. It wasn't until I was in my late teens and early twenties that I really started to give it serious thought and found myself taking pictures with photographers at the age of eighteen and nineteen.

127

I was working a nine-to-five job in the investment banking sales room. I was working in what was then called the secretarial pool. But the little whispers in my ear wanted me to get into the fashion industry and this would not be quiet. So, I reduced my hours and started some corporate modeling during the day. Then I took a step further and ended up leaving my job to have more time for modeling and started working at a restaurant as a hostess at night in Lower Manhattan.

And it was there that I was discovered, if you will. A woman who owned an agency (Lure, which is no longer in existence) was a customer at the restaurant. She asked if I was interested in modeling. I signed with her and worked with her for several months, just kind of getting my feet wet and learning the industry. I learned that your representation matters just as much as your ability to model.

I stayed with her for a few months and then I found better representation. I signed with Wilhelmina models and they're still around to this day. They were one of the top agencies back in the mid-to-late nineties. And then I went on to Ford Models, where I spent the majority of my career. Ford Models is one of the pioneers in the fashion industry. Jerry and Eileen Ford are responsible for so many of the tenets of the modeling industry.

I was always looking for what the next thing was for myself. I was very fortunate to be working consistently. I was extremely fortunate to get what is considered the "Super Bowl" of modeling: I landed a cosmetic campaign with Maybelline Cosmetics. I was the first African-American woman to land an exclusive contract with them and that's something that I continue to be very proud of.

Career Defining Moments

I didn't go the route that most models go. Number one, I was officially twenty-five when I started modeling full time, which was considered seventy-two in model years at the time. Another thing that I did that went against the grain was that all models at the time were advised to go and get their learning in Europe, living there for a year or two. I didn't want to do that. I had no interest in leaving New York and leaving my family, so I was able to have success without having gone and spent years overseas.

By the time I landed my cosmetic campaign in 1999 or 2000, I was in my early thirties. I found that going my own route and believing in myself and paving my own way was really working for me.

How Taking Risks Impacted Tomiko's Career Journey

If you were to ask me if I were a risk taker, my very practical, play-by-the-rules persona would say no, but I think that I've been a risk taker all along and I guess I wouldn't always have defined it as risk. I would have defined it as having gone my own way. So, going my own way to some may have been seen as taking a risk. So, yeah, at my core I guess I am a risk taker. But a risk taker in a different sense, like I'm not going to jump out of a plane! I'm not going to do anything to harm myself, but I am going to go in the direction that I feel is my calling or my truth, even if I don't have it all mapped out or even if everybody else has gone that way and it hasn't worked for them. I'm going to at least try it because I've not had my own experience and I'm going to come to my own conclusions.

Avoiding Responsibility for One's Career

One thing that comes to mind is lying about my age. I started, as I said, officially full time when I was 25 and my agent at the time told me, "You have to say you're 19." And I played along with that for 15 years because that's what I was told the industry standard was. And being an older woman, a more seasoned woman, was not going to sell products. Clients were not looking for you if you were over 25 or 30. So I definitely took the passenger route with not disclosing my age. And even sometimes, to the detriment of my expressions, whether I may have had an opinion about something, somebody who is 20 shouldn't be as informed as somebody who was in their mid-to-late twenties.

It was a very pivotal moment when I chose powerfully to no longer lie about my age. I have a women's empowerment group called the Tomiko Fraser Goddess Gathering, and it has been in existence for about 15 years. We were doing a gathering with young girls, aged eight, nine, eleven-year-old African American and Latina girls. And one of the girls innocently asked me, "Ms. Tomiko, how old are you?" I was about to go into my routine of lying about my age and give my model age. But I looked at her and I became present to my surroundings, whom I was talking with, and the purpose that I had aligned with at that point. I looked at her in front of that group of little girls and the entire group of women that were there with me and I said, "It's because of you that I'm no longer going to lie about my age. I am 40 years old." That was ten years ago. "I'm 40 years old and I understand that I can't sit here and tell you to be your truth and encourage you to be empowered and while continuing to lie about my age." So, from that day forward, much to my agent's dismay, I started to shout my age from the rooftops. Ever since I haven't stopped. I think I'm still doing it. I am 50 years old and I'm very proud of it.

The Formula for Owning Your Career

I cannot give a blanket statement for all career owners, but I would say as a model and working in the fashion industry, that owning your career is really being your truth. Yes, we are paid to be chameleons. We are paid to bend and shape and look and sell the way that our client desires of us. But my foundation is my truth, so that is the advice I give to just women in general, but models especially. Have other interests. Bring your full self to your career. It really all boils down to bringing your full self and being your truth. The days of lying about your age, to me, should be long gone. There's no shame in growing older. There's no shame in having a little more meat on your bones. There's no shame in having a few wrinkles, or a lot of wrinkles, or whatever. All the things that we have been told are not acceptable by whoever "they" are is not true. We've just been fed so many lies that we believe that they're the truth.

I stepped away from the modeling world due to my infertility and wanting to be at home to be with my boys for the first few years of their life, and I said, over and over again, "I don't want to return to it unless I can do something my full self." And that happened this January when I booked a consistent client that knows how old I am. I can wear my hair just the way that I want to, my body type was just fine and they're flexible with my schedule. I'm only working for them once a month right now. So, to be able to work in a field that I've loved for so many years but have had to compromise myself for, and then no longer have to compromise myself for and be exactly who I am, is the most fulfilling. I don't have any regrets because I learned so much having had to kind of find myself through all of that.

Key Relationships

I have been mostly responsible for my successes. I absolutely have the most amazing community of people around me who cheer me on, who give me a shoulder to cry on when I need it or a soft place to land when I just need to rest. But I have absolutely been responsible for the trajectory of my career, especially as of late.

I have nurtured the relationships that I am so grateful to have in my life, whether that be my husband, my children, my mother-in-love—I call her my mother-in-love and not my mother-in-law, because she is my heart— or my best friends, the community of women, my goddess sisters that I'm surrounded by. I nurture those relationships by showing up for them the way that they show up for me. I like to say we mirror each other. I'm very fortunate to be able to look around and look in the eyes of everybody around me, whether it be my brother or just everybody, and see that empowered spirit, that loving spirit, that "let's go get it" spirit. I don't have anybody who is resting on their laurels. Even if we're different ages or at different points in our careers or in our growth, everybody I'm surrounded by knows who they are and are striving to grow themselves more. So, I nurture those relationships by being my most authentic self, with myself and with them.

Mentoring and Sponsorships as Career Levers

I can speak more to mentors than I can to sponsors. I absolutely think that people can benefit from having a mentor. I don't know if you need one, I'm very aware of the words and language that I use, so I don't know if "need" is the word that I would personally use, but the possibilities to benefit from a mentor, whether they be a career mentor or somebody who is living a life with the vibrancy that you are after, absolutely. I have benefited from mentors throughout my life. I still continue to have mentors that I benefit from. So, I'm an advocate of mentors, for sure.

Sharing Career Successes

I share them via social media. But I share them with my community, my friends, my family, just by texting or calling. I may want to treat us all to lunch one day or I'm buying dinner, or we're taking a little trip here or there. I have learned not to hide my money. I learned this back when I had my Maybelline contract, because with a cosmetic campaign comes people knowing who you are. Up until then, I had not been sharing how much money I had been making, especially with my inner circle. I was making a lot of money and I thought, "Well, why am I hiding it? Why do we hide when we're doing well with our loved ones?" I got my head around the fact that by sharing what I was able to achieve, I may make possible the belief in someone else that they can do the same in what they're after. So now I share that, mostly with my inner circle. It's always a reminder or a spark to them to get on their path to their abundance. So, I speak it. I put it on social media, I do a dance about it. That how I share my successes.

Valuable Online Tools for Career Management

Facebook and Instagram have proven most beneficial in the sharing of my purpose, which is to empower women. So, I don't know if I would call that my career, but it definitely is my purpose. Has it benefited me financially? Possibly. I have become a regular model for Chico's. They use me on a regular basis and whenever I'm booked by Chico's, I post that on social media and I continue to get booked. People who follow me on social media will tag Chico's and say, "Thank you for using Tomiko." So, I'm sure that there's some co-mingling of my purpose and my career in there that I am benefiting from.

Career Advice

Someone asked me, "What would you do for the rest of your life if you never received dime for it?" And without hesitation I said, "Empower women." That's my driving force in life. And so, if you are someone who is pursuing a career, or considering a career change, or in a career that you're not sure about, ask yourself if you would be doing this thing that you're doing or that you want to do for the rest of your life, if you would not be paid a dime? And if your answer is no, you might want to just look at the why you are pursuing this career. Because I believe that with happiness comes a passion, enthusiasm, and joy. And yes, you can be making all the money in the world, but if you're miserable every day going to this job, then what's the point? You want to be doing something that brings you fulfillment, so I was blessed with that. As far as a career goes, really be clear on what brings you joy and what doesn't.

Make sure that you are passionate about what you are doing. And I am fully aware that not everybody is in their dream job at the moment. But you can find the joy, find the passion in what you're doing. Then you will start to attract to you, with your thoughts and your words and your actions, the career that you desire. If you constantly think of how miserable you are in your career, that is likely to be what you continue to experience. But if you start to speak of the career that you desire, think about it, see yourself doing it, be around people who are doing it, read books about it, you will really start to bring into your life all of the elements that will make that particular career a reality for you.

Eric Pliner
Chief Commercial Officer | Managing Director, Americas
YSC Consulting

I first met Eric Pliner back in my Diageo days. He was the consultant who I worked with to plan an Employee Resource Group Summit I was in charge of. I remember being impressed by Eric. He was easy to talk to and very sharp indeed. The planning process was fruitful and he delivered the education piece of the summit. It was such a great experience that we kept in touch after I left Diageo.

I will always be grateful to my old boss Lisa for connecting us. As I thought through people I wanted to profile, Eric came to mind. He is very humble and gracious and always willing to help. I know you'll benefit from hearing his story and the nuggets of wisdom that shine through in his profile.

The Story
I've been at YSC Consulting for eight years, working in the fields of leadership strategy, executive assessment, executive coaching, leadership development, team development, and inclusive leadership and diversity, but in a way that I never really knew existed before I joined this firm.

My role at YSC is the first role that I've held in the private sector. One day I got a call from a headhunter who said, "What do you think about consulting?" And I said, "I think it's the worst job in the world." It's living in airports and never getting to do anything in any real depth and not feeling tied to anything, and she said, "I think you should just go check out this company." I thought, well what do I have to lose? So, I went, visited YSC, and I fell in love and I thought, I have the opportunity to be a learner for the rest of my life by getting to visit any company I'm interested in and in any industry that I'm interested in.

Before I came here, I spent my entire career in government and in non-profit organizations.

I loved the idea of doing social change work through government. I thought there was something really powerful about being able to help people through existing government agencies, but doing something that was about creating change at the same time. And as it happened, when I finished my first government internship, the person I worked for decided to go back to graduate school, and that left a vacancy, and my timing was fortunate, and I was able to become a full-time coordinator of that program.

I had a side life, though, as a writer. So, as a creative outlet for a long time, I did a lot of volunteer work with community-based organizations. I spent three years on the committee that ran the Boston LGBT Pride Parade, and the third year was one of the hardest things I've ever done. I was the co-director of that committee. And when it was over I thought, I just want to do something for myself, for fun, with my friends, and so I got together a group of friends and I wrote a play. And we put on a play at a little theater in Boston, having no idea that that play would become commercially very successful, end up moving to New York, and end up being published and carried by a British licensing house forever after that.

Owning Your Career

Lifelong learning, owning your time, and I think there's something about regularly connecting with people who have very different life experiences, identities, expertise, ways of working, and ways of living in the world from yourself. Because I think the world is a lot broader and bigger than any of us typically realizes on an average day, and the more that we connect and extend our connections with people who are different from each of us in lots of different ways, the bigger, or the better the access we'll have to that bigger world. And that is awesome for building a career that's somewhat unexpected.

How Taking Risks Impacted Eric's Career Journey

I've taken a number of calculated risks along the way. I've never been the kind of person to say, I'm just going to throw everything in my imaginary truck and drive to another city and start a new life. I'm not that sort of wild risk taker. But, I have always thought about what would it be like to try something really different and to pick up a new part of life, and therefore, a new part of myself by being in a setting that's really unfamiliar. I don't think I'd be where I am if I hadn't taken some pretty big risks along the way, but they were all calculated, informed risks. They weren't arbitrary risks.

Avoiding Responsibility for One's Career

I have never been someone who's good about getting places on time. The boss I was working for at the time felt that any kind of lateness was a sign of disrespect and would not be tolerated. I remember coming in seven minutes late one day after the start of my "shift" and getting called into her office and being told if I wanted to continue working there, I would need to start arriving on time. And I said, "But I stayed three and a half hours late last night." And she said, "I don't care if you stayed all night. Your shift starts at 9:00 and you need to be here by then."

And I was so angry that I did not take responsibility for it at all. I felt like, well, screw this, you're not seeing the value that I'm contributing. "Would you rather have somebody who works hard or somebody who's here on time?" And she said to me, "I'd rather have both."

And I took no personal responsibility for it. I felt like I justified everything to myself, well, she doesn't know what really matters. But the truth is, this was the cultural norm that the leader of the organization was attempting to create. These were the conditions that she wanted, that she felt were right, and I certainly could've challenged that appropriately, but, instead, I acted out.

The Formula for Owning Your Career
The first is to commit to being a lifelong learner. I think recognizing that you can develop expertise in your field, but that none of us is ever really an expert is a great way to grow your career because you see possibility in things everywhere you turn.

I think the second thing is owning and managing your time. So, I've noticed that in my own career, and also with a lot of the executives that I coach, we become reliant on our assistants to manage our time or on others to schedule for us. I think this is the biggest secret to being able to own your career: owning and managing your time yourself. It doesn't mean you can't get help, but it means you want to be really thoughtful about, what kind of energy do I have at 9:00 o'clock in the morning? What kind of energy do I have at 3:00 o'clock in the afternoon? How am I going to feel if it takes me an hour to get somewhere and I only have 30 minutes? How am I going to feel if I'm rushing or if I'm tired?

It's about understanding your own energy and your emotions and then managing your time in service of those. Otherwise, you just can't get as much done in a day, which means you can't get as much done in a year, which means you don't get the same degree of opportunity in your career.

Key Relationships

There are mentors I had in my first job who are still people that I go to for advice now, 20 years later. I've been very, very fortunate to be the beneficiary of a huge amount of wisdom and generosity from people from all walks of life; I used to say all over the country, but now it's all over the world, some of whom have been my bosses, some of whom have been coworkers, some of whom have been peers, even some direct reports and some more junior folks. I just feel like the luckiest guy in the world when it comes to that stuff. People have had real generosity with me and maintaining those relationships over time has been incredibly important.

Mentoring and Sponsorships as Career Levers

I heard someone say once that everybody needs to have their own board of directors or their own kind of advisory board, and that is advice that I pass on often. But for much of my career and adult life, I hadn't thought of it that way. When I heard that I sat down and thought, well, at each part of my life, who have been my board of directors? Who have been my advisors? Who have been my mentors, or sponsors? Like I said, it was later when I first got a coach, but the first thing is the people from whom I think I learned the most may not have even realized that they were mentors to me. I think there's something to be gleaned by having as many people as possible who you're open to learning from. I think there's something about recognizing who evokes an emotional reaction in you, and not necessarily a positive one. And realizing that even the people who evoke the most intense negative reactions have something to teach us.

I think there's something about interacting as much as you can with people of different age ranges, life stages, and generations. So, I've found that when I spend time with people who are notably older or notably younger than me, that I learn a ton from them as mentors, that they just help me to see the world differently. I think there's something about asking lots of questions and about being willing to accept the generosity that other people offer to you, even if it isn't always packaged in the most generous way. The content of that package may still be incredibly generous.

I have had extraordinary mentors who I think were often very patient with me, even when maybe I didn't deserve that patience. Extraordinary people.

Sharing Career Successes

The things I'm really proud of, I share with my immediate family, with my husband, with my brother, with my parents, with one or two close friends. But I think, actually, quite a few people in my life would be very surprised by how much I do in many aspects of my career, because I don't share a lot of it.

Career Advice

- Become a really, really good listener.
- Ask lots of people lots of questions about their journeys, because you'll get lots of ideas about ways to craft your own that are pretty different from your own lived experience. There's just no way that any one of us can live lots of different experiences all at once, so, the best thing we can do is learn from lots of other people's experiences, and that means being a great questioner and a great listener.
- Meet and talk to as many people as you can. I think people love to talk about themselves. A mentor taught me this quite early on. So, if you are genuinely asking because you're curious, not because you have an ultimate goal in mind, you can learn so much by just asking people to tell you their story. People are often quite generous with their time, and all you have to do is ask and say thanks, and that goes a really long way.
- When you find something that interests you, read all about it, and figure out who in your network knows somebody who could tell you more about it or who could introduce you to somebody who could tell you more about it.

- Sketch out, for yourself, what are the experiences you want to have and then strategize about how you can create the relationships, or the opportunities to have those exposures and experiences. There's something about putting it down on paper that goes a long way towards making it manifest. Envisioning experiences can really help you to own your career because your career is really an aggregation of experiences rather than just a series of jobs.

Mohammed Murad
Entrepreneur
Past International President, Toastmasters International

I first met Mohammed when he was president of the Toastmasters organization. Toastmasters is a global non-profit organization that provides communication and leadership education and experience. I have a fond affection for Toastmasters, having been a member for over 10 years. I was fortunate to travel to Kuala Lumpur, Malaysia to attend the first conference being held outside of the United States and I got the opportunity to engage with the then-president Mohammed. I was immediately drawn to his leadership style and the warmth he exuded to everyone. Years later, I leveraged social media to connect with him to ask him to share his story. He was more than gracious to work with me. Below you will find Mohammed's heartwarming story.

The Story
My career includes 20 years with the Dubai Police Force. I am a serial entrepreneur and event management mogul with four companies under my leadership. I am Past International President of the Toastmasters International Organization.

Career Defining Moments
My first career defining moment was when I was studying in my local university and I suddenly decided that I wanted to go to the US to study. As I was applying for a scholarship, I came across the news that there was a cadet batch going into the police academy, and because my father was a police

144

officer, I had a certain attraction to the uniform. So, I decided to leave studying and join the police force. This was a life-changing perspective on what discipline means.

Another defining moment was when I got transferred from the Criminal Investigation Department to the Emergency Medical Department. If ever someone has moved from one end of the spectrum to another, this was it, from crimes to medicine, from streets to a leadership role. I was a member of a team of around ten officers in Criminal Investigation, while I was leading around 1000 in the Emergency Medical Services, and just the sheer responsibility of running the EMS for a whole city was such a defining moment.

Then I asked for voluntary retirement after 20 years of service. I made a total shift in career, as I had no idea what I was going to do. I started an event management company. I now run four companies.

Owning Your Career
I believe there is one single element that will allow you to become successful and take ownership of your career: self-confidence. This develops into a path, and the path develops into a vision, which shapes the career.

How Taking Risks Impacted Mohammed's Career Journey
My whole life was about taking risks, uncertainty, and lack of planning. But there is one thing that stayed consistent:

Once I took on a certain path, I made sure I did it well and followed through till the end. In other words, have faith and hope, and never give up.

Avoiding Responsibility for One's Career

I have learned that there will be times in life when we will need to say no. That does not in any way mean that we do not want to take on responsibilities, but means that we understand our priorities and are able to quantify our other responsibilities. I have turned down a couple of requests to be on the boards of some organizations, and a few job offers, when I was available on the job market a long time ago.

The Formula for Owning Your Career

A career is doing what I love, be it a job, or just a lifestyle that facilitates living comfortably. Here are the steps: Be able to notice opportunities, take the ones that appeal to you most, and once on the path, follow through no matter what challenges come into that path.

Key Relationships

I believe every single relationship plays a role in success, regardless whether it has affected us positively or negatively. There are two ways we benefit from relationships: understanding how to deal with different personalities and being responsible for the positive outcome of the relationship. Again, we are responsible for our relationships we are in, not the other person.

Mentoring and Sponsorships as Career Levers

We are community-based creatures. We need people to learn from. Regardless of what title we have for them, they are there to take us through. The most powerful ones were what I call "undercover mentors." They are the ones I choose to follow, understand how they do things, and study their perspective of success. These could be any family members, friends, or experts in any field. The important aspect for me would be that they are unannounced. Formal mentoring relationships do not work for me.

Sharing Career Successes

I talk to anyone who wants to learn from my experience.

Valuable Online Tools for Career Management

Being able to tap into research resources and online courses have been and still are an integral part of my life. I will not name any because it is different for each one of us, and we will need to identify the ones that work for us.

Career Advice

- Always strive to become a better you; the career will be taken care of along the path.

Laura Skandera Trombley
President
University of Bridgeport

I met Laura earlier this year at a panel discussion on race relations in Norwalk, Connecticut. She was the last of the panelists to speak and her impassioned message spoke volumes to me as a fellow mom. I believed that she'd do her darndest to create change in her position. I found her to be genuine, authentic, gracious, and full of wisdom after hearing her speak for five minutes. Her story is inspiring and her advice for success is compelling to stay the course, do the work no one else wants to, and be successful. I know you will enjoy reading her profile.

The Story
I went to college in California, at Pepperdine and USC, and then I had the opportunity while I was in my PhD program to live and teach in Europe for a few years. I came back and graduated with my PhD and decided that I wanted to become a Twain scholar and thought moving near Hartford would be a good idea. The best position I could find was at SUNY Potsdam, and I spent seven years there. I moved into administration there and had my son, then accepted a position as dean of the faculty at Coe College in Cedar Rapids, Iowa.

After five years, I was recruited by various colleges and accepted a position at Pitzer College, where I was president for 13 years. I decided I'd step out of higher education for a little while and was president of the Huntington Library for two years. But I missed Higher Education and decided to accept a position as President at the University of Bridgeport.

In all of those instances, I always saw a particular issue or situation that I thought I could improve to add value to the institution. I always liked institutions that had a series of complex issues that needed to be sorted out because I like putting together puzzles, and I very much enjoy strategic thinking. I think that was probably the reason why I made each one of my moves.

How Taking Risks Impacted Laura's Career Journey

I think it's been in many ways all about risk. I've never taken a position where it looked as though it was without any risk. I've often been at institutions that had immediate problems or issues that had to be rectified and it was a risky thing to do. If I was risk averse, I probably would have stayed as a professor at SUNY Potsdam, Coe College, or Pitzer College with tenure. I would have had a job for the rest of my life, and I would have been very secure. I think what motivates me is the changing environment and one where it keeps unfolding. It isn't so certain. I find that to be of greater interest. I'd say a lot of what I've done has had a fairly high degree of risk attached to it.

The Formula for Owning Your Career

One, believe in yourself and be focused; and two, work with great people. People are everything. Your team is everything. Often, I think there's a general consensus that everything takes money; that all issues can be solved with money. That isn't the case. Strategy wins over money every day. It's figuring out how to get to the desired end in a way that has more of a collective ethos rather than if I just had a million dollars, everything would be great because I can think of many institutions that have considerable endowments that are perhaps in some ways the least entrepreneurial or the least interesting. They're in a kind of steady state. I think a lot of innovation comes from places where they're having to figure things out because they don't have an enormous amount of flexibility when it comes to budget.

Mentoring and Sponsorships as Career Levers
I think that's a huge part of any person's success, is that they have had a series of people who have pushed them and inspired them, and in some cases, convinced them, to try things that left to themselves, they never would have had the confidence to try. I was very fortunate when I was an undergraduate that I had a faculty member who really believed in me, greatly encouraged me, and really went to bat for me when I was at the point of graduation and trying to figure out what to do. It's because of him that I received a scholarship for my Master's degree.

When I was in the PhD program, I had another faculty mentor who's still alive, and he used to talk to me about places where I should have my work published and books that I should write. I would think he was crazy. No way I can see that. Look at me. His faith in me was just amazing, absolutely ironclad. Those are the people who have a profound influence upon you. I think if you speak to people who've had some measure of success, whether it's a family member or a professional colleague or a teacher, they will always be able to identify somebody.

Sharing Career Successes

One of the things that I've done, which in part I think is because I come from a scholarly background and I've worked a lot in archives and I like just saving data, is I've created a website that lists all of the things that I've done because I found that it makes things very easy to keep track of. Also, I think it's helpful in letting people know the kind of professional career I've had and the different aspects of my professional portfolio. I have maintained that.

I learned long ago, even though I didn't realize this at the time, that when I would teach a class, go to a conference, or speak to students, students look at you and you're put together. You look very professional. They assume that your life has been one path and that you've always been successful. They think you've always been together and that your life is always well organized. Everything has gone according to plan. I talk about my career and my path. My past includes every kind of service position imaginable. I've directed traffic at construction sites. I was a housekeeper. I was a maid. I was a waitress. I was a taxi driver. I worked constantly because I've been self-supporting since the age of 20. I didn't come from a place of privilege. I didn't come from a place of wealth and nobody gave me financial backing. I ate cup ramen for many, many, many years.

Career Advice

I had a very, very bright student when I was at Pitzer College, and she was endlessly in trouble, always in trouble. She would always wind up in my office, and I would talk to her. She would start fights and she'd do all these kinds of things. I said, "Look, you're a very intelligent person so you get to make the choice. You can use your intelligence to make trouble and I can tell you your future right here, or you can use your intelligence in a way that is going to help you move forward within our system. Then, you're going to have amazing options, but the choice ultimately is yours. You get to make that choice. It would be really tragic for an intelligent woman like yourself to choose the lesser path. That's a decision that you have to make."

It's also always good to have a group of professionally successful people who you can go to for advice. I know that when I've contemplated making moves, I always reached out to a particular group of people and discussed what I'm thinking of with them before I do it. It's also really important that you keep learning about whatever it is that you want to do, that you're constantly informing yourself, that you become your own best student, and that you don't stop trying to learn more about whatever it is that you want to do. The most successful people are the people who are constantly taking in information, looking at it critically, figuring out what works for them, discarding the rest, and moving forward. I'd say those are two things that are really important.

Harry Rilling
Mayor
City of Norwalk

Harry Rilling has been the Mayor of Norwalk, Connecticut since 2013. I first encountered the Mayor at close proximity at a church service entitled "Justice Sunday." It was an important event focused on important conversations and actions around peace. I noticed that the Mayor was very pleasant and welcoming after his speech. I am drawn to authentic people and so I made a mental note that at some point, I might want to do some diversity work with the city and that the Mayor would be a good contact to have. Fast forward years later, I reached out and requested an interview and to my delight he agreed to let me interview him. I was not disappointed. Mayor Rilling's story is another inspiring one. I felt fortunate to learn more about his journey.

The Story

I was born and raised in Norwalk. And in 1967, I was either going to be drafted into the military during the Vietnam War or I was going to enlist. I decided that the better track for me would be to have some control over my future. And I decided to enroll in the Navy for four years. I was guaranteed a training program, a school that I could go to that would give me some skills.

My father died when I was very young and my mother could not afford to send me to college. My mom was working two jobs. So, I didn't really apply myself in high school. When I was coming out of the Navy, my brother, who was in the police department in Norwalk, asked me what I was going to do. And I said, "I really don't know." I was a radioman in the Navy. But he asked me if I'd be interested in joining the police department. So, I said, "Sure. Why not?" And so, I joined the police department.

It was in the Navy that I started recognizing the importance of education. They put me in charge of 80 recruits right away. I organized study groups so we could all learn together and try to work together to increase the scores on our tests and to pass all the tests that we needed to pass.

So then when I got out of the Navy and I joined the police department, I kind of did the same thing in the academy where we held study groups and tested each other and so forth. Because I could see that having work groups like that together would be better off for everybody.

I enrolled in college while I was in the police department and started working towards a bachelor's degree in criminal justice. And I took the promotional examinations. I started as a patrolman. Got promoted to detective. Got promoted to sergeant. Got promoted to lieutenant.

In 1989, I completed my undergraduate work at Iona College in New Rochelle and graduated with a Master's degree from the University of New Haven. By that time, I had received a promotion to deputy chief in 1987 and then to chief in 1995. So, I went through the ranks in the police department.

My mom died the week after I graduated from the police academy. She had been proud to see me join the police department. One of my favorite pictures is my first day in uniform with my arm around my mom as I'm walking, getting ready to go for my first day on the job.

How Taking Risks Impacted Harry's Career Journey

It was 1978 when I went to Florida and I was 31. And my brother-in-law in Florida owned a Century 21 real estate office. And he told me, "I think you'd be a good real estate salesman." So those were the circumstances when I took a leave of absence from the police department.

In Florida, I went through a course to get my real estate license. And I think at that time it was a 60-hour course. So, I went through it and then I applied for my real estate license. I actually got a 98 out of 100 on the test. And at the time it was the highest score of anybody who had gone through the Century 21 course.

So, I stayed there in real estate for a period of time. At that time, I was married and had three children. I did really well for the first couple of months. I brought in a lot of money in commissions for my office and for myself.

It was a risk involving the family. I was trying to put the family in the situation where we could have a good environment, a good income, and a nice location. I had family down there. So, it was kind of an exciting thing to do.

I came back to Connecticut after my leave of absence from the police department was up and I remember distinctly I went to open a file cabinet to get a file on a case and it was just like, "I'm back here." And I'm thinking I made the wrong decision.

But I picked myself up, studied really hard and took the sergeant's test again and did really well. And got promoted. Then I was a sergeant for two years.

Avoiding Responsibility for One's Career

Back in the '70s, I was a detective and I had taken a sergeant's exam. I finished first on the detective's exam I took and I was promoted right away. And along came the sergeant's exam within maybe six, eight months. And I felt I finished so high on the detective's exam, I really didn't need to study and apply myself for the sergeant's exam. I was kind of ambivalent. I thought I would do really well. I came in 17th on the sergeant's exam and there was no way I was going to get promoted. I think that kind of knocked the wind out of my sails a little bit.

The Formula for Owning Your Career

Motivation is something that is inside of you. If you're motivated, you realize there are no shortcuts. If not, you sit back and want people to hand you something. You have to be motivated. You have to do everything you can to get to where you want to be. And you have to have a plan.

My plan earlier on was to become a sergeant in the detective bureau. But things don't always go according to plan and the only job I *never* had in the police department was sergeant in the detective bureau.

I ended up with virtually every other job that you could possibly have. But I saw my career as advancing me to a position where I could have an impact and make the necessary improvements and changes that I saw were needed in the police department. I could have a better position from which to do that.

The only thing I can say that really got me there was hard work and commitment to achieve the goals that I had set for myself.

It's kind of interesting because I've looked back and thought about who might have been kind of a role model for me. But I didn't really have any adult male role models that I could reach out to. The police department has lots of competitive examinations so you're competing with others. They're certainly not going to help you in any way. I wanted to be in a position of leadership so I could make my mark and pretty much self-actualized where I wanted to be.

Key Relationships

My success team consists of my wife, my chief of staff, my city clerk, and my counsel. They act in my best interest and I use their expertise.

Mentoring and Sponsorships as Career Levers

Former Mayors Frank Zillo, Bill Collins, and Alex Knopf were a part of my campaign team. Bill put the idea in my head to run for Mayor. He was my champion. I had a brain trust and we met weekly to talk about where we were going. Senator Bob Duff was a part of that team too.

Career Advice

- Remember failure is an orphan. Success has a million parents.
- Be yourself, know your limitations, never stop learning, and respect people.
- Use the expertise of people around you.
- Don't overrule unless you know you're right.
- Learn from the mistakes of the past. Don't be afraid to take ownership of those mistakes.
- Disagree behind closed doors.
- Stand up for strong convictions.
- Be prepared to do what you think is right.
- Foster collaboration. No one can do everything but everyone can do something.

8 HOW TO CREATE YOUR 90-DAY ROADMAP

As I think through the requirements for successfully owning your career, I am reminded of the late Napoleon Hill's book *Think and Grow Rich.* In the last year, I have been reintroduced to the book and I'm a believer in the influence the book can have on your career success.

The principles are solid and they work in keeping you focused on achieving your goals.

The key things I recommend from the book are:

1. Ensure your self-confidence remains solid. Do recite the self-confidence formula daily to ensure that your mindset game is up and you are well fueled to stay your path and achieve your successes.
2. Find your success squad. Find a mastermind group to support you on your journey. If you can't find one that meets your needs, create your own. Remember we talked about creating opportunities in earlier chapters.
3. Create a solid affirmation for yourself. Get clear on what it is you want and then create a solid affirmation that you repeat daily.

4. Allow yourself time to think through what you want and plan accordingly.

When you think of an action plan for your next 90 days, think "development plan." I know I kind of hate the words development plan from my corporate days but in retrospect, I can see the value of having such a document as a tool for success. I had a clear plan for achieving my project management professional certification and I followed it to a tee and guess what? It worked. How about we say professional development plan. That one word just makes it sound better, doesn't it? It's like adding frosting to your cupcake or cheese to your eggs.

As previously mentioned, it is important to create a plan of action to bring about the changes you seek.

There is power in the written plan, indeed. So, my dear reader, be the driver in this instance and get your plan written down.

To get started with your plan, answer the following:

What do you want?

Examples:
- I want a new job
- I want to get promoted

- I want to work internationally
- I want to gain a sponsor
- I want a mentor
- I want to build my personal brand
- I want to gain more speaking opportunities at work
- I want to gain more speaking opportunities externally
- I want to be my own boss

When do you want it?

Who do you need to help you get it?

I am a fan of the From/To template. I've seen it used in business and I know it's applicable here as well. Where are you coming from and where do you want to go? It provides a really good context for your 90-day plan.

Here is a high-level example of a plan that might be created.

Goal:	From:	To:	How
I want to get promoted to the leadership team in my current organization	Manager	Director	• Find out the requirements to gain promotion! • Audit myself again for said requirements. • Make a plan for addressing the gaps. • Demonstrate and track performance requirements. • Find sponsors to support my goal. • Have the right conversations. • Communicate effectively

9 CAREER RESOURCES

Books:
- *Think and Grow Rich* by Napoleon Hill
- *Never Eat Alone: And Other Secrets to Success, One Relationship at a Time* by Keith Ferrazzi
- *Build Your Dream Network: Forging Powerful Relationships In A Hyper-Connected World* by Kelly Hoey
- *Brag!: The Art of Tooting Your Own Horn without Blowing It* by Peggy Klaus
- *Feel the Fear and Do It Anyway* by Susan Jeffers
- *Achievement Unlocked: Strategies to Set your Own Goals and Manifest Them* by Simone E. Morris

Sites:
- Blogs are a valuable resource for providing educational awareness on career management. Check out articles on Glassdoor, The Ladders, Indeed, and more to solidify your toolkit for successfully owning your career.
- LinkedIn, a global career management platform, has 500 million users. It's worthwhile to leverage the site to build your personal brand and demonstrate your thought leadership.

Podcasts:

- Please continue the learning by subscribing to the Power of Owning Your Career podcast. You will continue to be inspired by listening to many more inspiring stories to support you on your career journey. Visit http://www.simonemorris.com/the-power-of-owning-your-career-podcast/ for more information.

10 CONCLUSION

The bottom line is that you are responsible for your career. I know first-hand because of my personal experiences and others I have observed and what has been conveyed to me from the 14 leaders I interviewed. These leaders all persevered, they gave back, and they took on new experiences without knowing how in all cases. In some cases, they took jobs no one else wanted, some attributed being in the right place at the right time with a willingness to embrace risk for growth…and you know what? They won.

Whatever you do, make the time to get clear on where you want to go in your career, create a plan to do so, and build a solid support team to help you along this journey.

Throughout *The Power of Owning Your Career*, you've had an opportunity to learn various perspectives on the formula for owning your career. No doubt this is valuable input to personalize and bolster your own formula. You no longer have to be happy with things happening that you're not thrilled about. You are empowered to take action and make life-changing decisions where you can be happy with the outcome realized. It is your roadmap to design. You have the keys to your success.

Go forth knowing you can powerfully own your career.

Get in the driver's seat; your car is waiting!

ABOUT THE AUTHOR

Simone Morris is CEO of Simone Morris Enterprises LLC, a certified minority and woman-owned business enterprise that provides consulting, training, career coaching, and speaking services.

The mission of the company is to empower women to succeed, enabling a life designed on their terms. Her company's signature *My Life My Way* retreat workshop runs for two days annually and focuses on visioning, education, action planning, and relationship building. Additionally, the company offers women an opportunity to continue the learning and provides support in reaching their goals by taking part in mastermind groups, training, and high-performance coaching.

Ms. Morris is an award-winning diversity and inclusion leader who has been recognized by Diversity Best Practices, Diversity MBA, and her former employer. Her background includes over two decades in Corporate America, spanning information technology, commercial strategy, and human resources. She has extensive leadership experience and holds an MBA from the University of Connecticut. She is a certified coach as well as a certified Project Management Professional. She is also an adjunct faculty member for the American Management Association. She is the author of *Achievement Unlocked: Strategies to Set Goals and Manifest Them.* Her message has been shared at conferences, universities, and corporations.

She previously served on the Board for the Women's Mentoring Network, a non-profit organization that provides career, educational and personal resources that lead to the economic empowerment of low-income women and their families.

WORKING WITH SIMONE

There are ample opportunities to work with Simone. Those opportunities include:

- High Performance Career Coaching
- Speaking Engagements
- Training
- Diversity and Inclusion Consulting

Contact Information:
smorris@simonemorris.com
929-399-6241
www.simonemorris.com
www.mylifemywayretreat.com

Made in the USA
Middletown, DE
21 December 2018